The Myth of Ownership

The Myth of Ownership

Taxes and Justice

LIAM MURPHY &
THOMAS NAGEL

OXFORD
UNIVERSITY PRESS
2002

BIB ID: 286473

OXFORD
UNIVERSITY PRESS
Oxford   New York

Auckland   Bangkok   Buenos Aires   Cape Town   Chennai
Dar es Salaam   Delhi   Hong Kong   Istanbul   Karachi   Kolkata
Kuala Lumpur   Madrid   Melbourne   Mexico City   Mumbai   Nairobi
São Paulo   Shanghai   Singapore   Taipei   Tokyo   Toronto

and an associated company in Berlin

Copyright © 2002 by Oxford University Press, Inc.

Published by Oxford University Press, Inc.
198 Madison Avenue, New York, New York 10016

www.oup.com.

Oxford is a registered trademark of Oxford University Press

Library of Congress Cataloging-in-Publication Data
Murphy, Liam B., 1960–
The myth of ownership : taxes and justice / by Liam Murphy and Thomas Nagel.
p. cm.
Includes bibliographical references and index.
ISBN 0-19-515016-3
1. Tax incidence—United States.   2. Taxation—Social aspects—United States.
3. Distributive justice—United States.   I. Nagel, Thomas, 1937–   II. Title.
HJ2322.A3 M87 2002
336.2'00973—dc21   2001046486

1 3 5 7 9 8 6 4 2

Printed in the United States of America
on acid-free paper

Preface

In the fall term of 1998, we gave a joint seminar at NYU Law School on Justice and Tax Policy. When the term was over, it occurred to us that we might have the material for a book on the subject. We began writing in the summer of 1999, and this is the result.

We owe a large debt of gratitude to the participants in that seminar, both students and faculty, who helped us to explore an unfamiliar field and unfamiliar material. Our students gave us valuable critical responses and made the course a pleasure to teach.

We cannot begin to thank sufficiently for their indispensable help six present and past members of the NYU tax faculty, who with patience and generosity took on the education of a couple of amateurs: David Bradford, Noel Cunningham, Deborah Paul, Deborah Schenk, Daniel Shaviro, and Miranda Stewart. In addition, Barbara Fried was visiting NYU from Stanford the year we taught our seminar, and her advice and criticism have been enormously helpful throughout.

After we began writing, we got valuable responses when we presented parts of the material to various audiences: to the Tax Policy Colloquium at NYU conducted by David

Bradford and Daniel Shaviro, to the Law and Philosophy Colloquium at NYU, and to audiences at Harvard, Duke, The University of North Carolina at Chapel Hill, University College London, the Central European University in Budapest, and the Centro di Ricerca e Studi sui Diritti Umani in Rome.

We have benefited from written comments on various parts of the manuscript from Janos Kis, Marjorie Kornhauser, and Daniel Shaviro, and also from conversation with Ronald Dworkin and Lewis Kornhauser. We are exceptionally grateful to four people who gave us detailed comments on the whole manuscript: Barbara Fried, Eric Rakowski, Joel Slemrod, and Lawrence Zelenak. Their penetrating and trenchant criticisms and constructive suggestions have allowed us to improve the book immeasurably. Without the generous attention of these experts on the law and economics of taxes we could not have produced a halfway respectable result.

Both of us received research support during the writing of the book from the Filomen D'Agostino and Max E. Greenberg Faculty Research Fund of New York University Law School. During the 2000–2001 academic year Liam Murphy was a Fellow of the National Humanities Center.

We started out by calling the book *Justice in Taxation*, but decided later on this more provocative title, partly at the urging of our editor at Oxford University Press, Dedi Felman. It seemed a good idea to make clear in the title where we stood. But the book is not designed just to defend a thesis: It aims to provide an accurate guide to the issues and to the arguments on all sides, and we hope that even those who disagree with us about the correct approach to justice in tax policy will find their views fairly represented here.

New York, September, 2001   L. M.
                                                               T. N.

Contents

The Myth of Ownership

1

Introduction

In a capitalist economy, taxes are not just a method of payment for government and public services: They are also the most important instrument by which the political system puts into practice a conception of economic or distributive justice. That is why they arouse such strong passions, fueled not only by conflicts of economic self-interest but also by conflicting ideas of justice or fairness.

A graph showing the variation in marginal tax rates, or the percentage of income paid in taxes by different income groups, or the percent of the total tax burden carried by different segments of the population, is bound to get a rise out of almost anybody. While people don't agree about what is fair, there is a widespread sense that tax policy poses the issue of fairness in an immediate way. How much should be paid by whom, and for what purposes, what should be exempt from taxation or deductible from the tax base, what kinds of inequalities are legitimate in after-tax income or in the taxes paid by different people—these are morally loaded and hotly disputed questions about our obligations to one another through the fiscal operations of our common government.

Yet while it is clear that these questions have to do with justice, they have generated less sophisticated discussion, from a moral point of view, than other public questions that have a moral dimension—questions about freedom of expression, pornography, abortion, equal protection, affirmative action, the regulation of sexual conduct, religious liberty, euthanasia, and assisted suicide. While there has been a great deal of debate over socioeconomic justice at the most abstract level in recent years, since John Rawls's *A Theory of Justice* returned the scholarly world's attention to the subject, those arguments about general theories of justice have made relatively little contact with the ideologically loaded battles over tax policy that are the bread and butter of politics.

This is partly because fiscal policy involves large empirical uncertainties about the economic consequences of different choices, and it is hard to disentangle the disagreements about justice from the disagreements about what will happen. A theory of justice cannot by itself approve or condemn a tax cut, for example; it requires some estimate of the effects of such a change on investment, employment, government revenue, and the distribution of after-tax income. With the prominent issues of individual rights, by contrast, the moral dimension can be more easily distinguished, even if empirical questions are also involved.

Another reason for the difference may be that tax battles are fought out in electoral politics, where rhetorical appeals are overwhelmingly important, rather than in the courts, where detailed and time-consuming argument is more welcome. Certainly the role of U.S. courts, in defining individual rights through constitutional interpretation, has had a large influence on the introduction of moral and political theory into those other areas of public debate.

Whatever the reason, there seems to us to be a gap or at least an underpopulated area in philosophical discussion of the ethical dimensions of public policy, and this book is intended to make a start at occupying it. This is especially important at a time when serious public discussion of economic justice has been largely displaced by specious rhetoric about tax fairness. We want to describe the important issues, criticize some previous approaches, and defend conclusions to the extent that we can arrive at them.

Many of the issues that crop up in political debate have to do with the design of the tax system, but there is also a large question about its purpose—about what kinds of things a government should be levying taxes to pay for. Public goods like defense and domestic order or security are uncontroversial, but beyond that minimum there is controversy. To what extent should education be financed out of tax revenues, or health care, or mass transportation, or the arts? Should taxation be used to redistribute resources from rich to poor, or at least to alleviate the condition of those who are unable to support themselves adequately because of disability or unemployment or low earning capacity?

There are questions about the best form of taxation—whether it should be levied on individuals or businesses or on particular economic transactions, as by a sales tax or value-added tax. Should the base be wealth and property or the flow of resources over time—and in the latter case, should the measure be income or consumption? How should the tax system treat the transfer of resources within families and across generations, particularly at death?

There are issues about what should not be taxed—what level of minimum income, if any, should be exempt from taxation, for example, and what types of expenditures should be tax deductible or yield tax credits. There is the perennial issue of proportional or "flat" versus progressive taxes and of the appropriate degree of progressivity. And there are familiar questions about differences in the treatment of different categories of taxpayers—the married and the unmarried, for example, or homeowners and renters—and about what is required to justify such differences.

Finally, there is the question whether a general presumption has to be overcome against taxation and in favor of leaving resources in the private hands of those who have created or acquired them—a presumption against "big government" and in favor of allowing people to do what they want with the resources that they have acquired through participation in a free market economy. If there were such a presumption, or prima facie case against, it would mean that the case for supporting various projects and aims out of tax revenue would have to be that much stronger.

Many of these questions arise about taxes at every level—national, state, and local—so taxes are at the heart of morally charged politics wherever elections are held, and sometimes they even form the subject of direct referenda. There are other ways of raising money that complicate the picture, such as import duties, license fees, tolls, state-run lotteries, and of course borrowing, but we will leave them aside. In a nonsocialist economy, without public ownership of the means of production, taxes and government expenditures are the primary focus of arguments over economic justice.

These arguments take us into the territory of more abstract controversies of political and social philosophy, and it is the bearing of those philosophical controversies on tax policy that we will explore. They all come out of the attempt to describe the rights and duties of a democratic state with respect to its citizens, and the rights and duties of those citizens with respect to the state and to one another.

Limited democratic government constrains individuals in certain respects, leaves them free in others, and provides them with certain benefits, both positive and negative. It usually creates those benefits by means of constraints, whether it is keeping the peace or maintaining public safety or raising revenue for child care, public education, and old-age benefits. Disagreements over the legitimate scope of government benefit and constraint, and over the way that scope is affected by individual rights, are likely to underlie differences over taxation, even when they are not made explicit. These are disagreements about the extent and limits of our collective authority over one another through our common institutions.

It is now widely believed that the function of government extends far beyond the provision of internal and external security through the prevention of interpersonal violence, the protection of private property, and defense against foreign attack. The question is how far. Few would deny that certain positive public goods, such as universal literacy and a protected environment, that cannot be guaranteed by private action, require government intervention. There are political differences about the appropriate level of public provision of such goods. But what arouses the most controversy is the use of government power not only to provide what is good for everybody but also to provide extra resources for those who are worse off, on the ground that certain sorts of social and economic inequality are unjust or otherwise bad, and that we have an obligation to our fellow citizens to rectify or alleviate those problems.

Much of the controversy has to do with the justice or injustice of outcomes produced by a market economy—the relation between market outcomes and reward for productive contribution, the degree to which the determinants of economic success or failure are arbitrary from a moral point of view. What is the moral basis for a right to hold on to one's earnings? Where the economy is largely private and the government democratic, tax policy will be the site where moral disagreements about these matters are fought out.

Since each of us is both a private individual, entering as a participant into the market economy, and a citizen who participates, at least potentially, in the process of public choice through politics, we have to combine our convictions about social justice and political legitimacy with our more personal motives, in arriving at a stable view of what we want government to do. When we decide whether to favor or oppose a tax cut, we think about its effect on our own disposable income, as well as about its broader social and economic consequences. The fact that tax policy is not set by forces outside the society but must be in some way chosen by those within it, as the political outcome of inevitable deep disagreements, makes the subject all the more complicated. The accommodation between personal and public motives in democratic politics is therefore an important part of the discussion.

Before getting to moral and political philosophy, however, we need to say something about the way evaluative questions have been treated, and to a considerable extent still are treated, in the traditional tax policy literature. Certain concepts have been developed specifically for application to the evaluation of tax policy: vertical equity, horizontal equity, the benefit principle, equal sacrifice, ability to pay, and so forth. We will begin by examining these concepts and will try to explain why they do not adequately capture the considerations that ought to enter into the normative assessment of tax policy.

If there is a dominant theme that runs through our discussion, it is this: Private property is a legal convention, defined in part by the tax system; therefore, the tax system cannot be evaluated by looking at its impact on private property, conceived as something that has independent existence and validity. Taxes must be evaluated as part of the overall system of property rights that they help to create. Justice or injustice in taxation can only mean justice or injustice in the system of property rights and entitlements that result from a particular tax regime.

The conventional nature of property is both perfectly obvious and remarkably easy to forget. We are all born into an elaborately structured legal system governing the acquisition, exchange, and transmission of property rights, and ownership comes to seem the most natural thing in the world. But the modern economy in which we earn our salaries, own our homes, bank accounts, retirement savings, and personal possessions, and in which we can use our resources to consume or invest, would be impossible without the framework provided by government supported by taxes. This doesn't mean that taxes are beyond evaluation—only that the target of evaluation must be the system of property rights that they make possible. We cannot start by taking as given, and neither in need of justification nor subject to critical evaluation, some initial allocation of possessions—what people originally own, what is theirs, prior to government interference.

Any convention that is sufficiently pervasive can come to seem like a law of nature—a baseline for evaluation rather than something to be evaluated. Property rights have always had this delusive effect. Slaveowners in the American South before the Civil War were indignant over the violation of their property rights that was entailed by efforts to prohibit the importation of slaves into the territories—not to mention stronger abolitionist efforts, like helping runaway slaves escape to Canada. But property in slaves was a legal creation, protected by the U.S. Constitution, and the justice of such forms of interference with it could not be assessed apart from the justice of the institution itself.

Most conventions, if they are sufficiently entrenched, acquire the appearance of natural norms; their conventionality becomes invisible. That is part of what gives them their strength, a strength they would lack if they were not internalized in that way. For another pervasive example, consider the conventions governing the different roles of men and women in any society. There may be good or bad reasons for the existence of such conventions, but it is essential, in evaluating them, to avoid the mistake of offering as a justification precisely those ostensibly "natural" rights or norms that are in fact just the psychological effects of internalizing the convention itself. If women are always treated as subordinate to men, the perception inevitably arises that submissiveness is a natural feminine trait and virtue, and this in turn is used to justify male dominance. Aristotle mistook the consequences of an institution for its natural basis in this way when he argued that certain people were natural slaves, and also in his claims about women.[1] To appeal to the consequences of a convention or social institution as a fact of nature which provides the justification for that convention or institution is always to argue in a circle.

In the case of taxes and property, the situation is more complicated, and it can be even more absurd. The feeling of natural entitlement produced by an unreflective sense of what are in fact conventionally defined property rights can encourage complacency about the status quo, as something more or less self-justifying. But it can also give rise to an even more confused criticism of the existing system on the ground that it violates natural property rights, when, in fact, these "natural" rights are merely misperceptions of the legal consequences of the system itself. It is illegitimate to appeal to a baseline of property rights in, say, "pretax income," for the purpose of evaluating tax policies, when all such figures are the product of a system of which taxes are an inextricable part. One can neither justify nor criticize an economic regime by taking as an independent norm something that is, in fact, one of its consequences.

This is, as we have said, completely obvious, but as we will try to show, it is easy to forget. The appropriate form of a system of property rights and its shaping by tax policy is a difficult question, and to address it requires that we take up a number of ethical issues about individual liberty, interpersonal obligation, and both collective and personal responsibility. Property rights are not the starting point of this subject but its conclusion.

While we hope the theoretical questions we discuss will have general application, we are going to conduct the discussion with reference to more or less familiar American examples. And we will talk mostly about federal rather than state and local taxation, and about taxes on individuals rather than corporations—even though the federal personal income tax plus Social Security and Medicare taxes amount to only about half of total tax revenues in the United States. Specific taxes must, of course, be assessed in the context of the whole economic picture, including other taxes. But the general issues we are concerned with arise everywhere.

The book is organized as follows. In the next two chapters we discuss general principles, first as they have been understood by tax theorists and then as they have been understood by philosophers. Chapter 2 examines the main criteria proposed in the tax policy literature to evaluate the fairness of taxes. This work comes from the disciplines of economics and law, and it has by now a considerable history. Chapter 3 then provides a critical survey of the diverse theories of social, political, and economic justice, developed in discussion among moral and political philosophers over a still longer history, that have implications for how tax policy should be evaluated—even if those implications have not always been explicitly drawn. The two approaches are quite different, in spite of the variety to be found within each of them. In chapter 4, we explain a fundamental distinction between two functions of taxation, which is important in identifying the values that should bear on its multiple effects. Chapters 5, 6, and 7 take up from the standpoint of justice three central issues about the design of the tax system: the tax base (what should be taxed); whether taxes should be progressive, and if so to what degree; and taxation of inherited wealth. Chapter 8 discusses some specific charges of discrimination among taxpayers by certain forms of tax. Throughout the book we try to present fairly a range of competing views about all these questions, without concealing our own sympathies. In the concluding chapter, we draw together the results of the preceding discussion, summarize our views, and say what practical policies we think they imply under the political constraints of the real world.

2

Traditional Criteria of Tax Equity

I. Political Morality in Tax Policy: Fairness

It has been recognized for a long time that tax policy must take account of political morality, or justice.[1] Though economic theory provides essential information about the likely effects of different possible schemes of taxation, it cannot by itself determine a choice among them. Anyone who advocates the tax policy that is, simply, "best for economic growth" or "most efficient" must provide not only an explanation of why the favored policy has those virtues, but also an argument of political morality that justifies the pursuit of growth or efficiency regardless of other social values.

Apart from economic efficiency, the social value that has traditionally been given weight in tax design is fairness; the task of the tax designer is to come up with a scheme that is both efficient and fair.[2] Fairness, in the traditional conception, is thought of specifically as a standard for evaluating differences in the tax treatment of different people: the principle that like-situated persons must be burdened equally and relevantly unlike persons unequally.

Historically, much of the discussion of justice in taxation has taken the form of attempts to interpret this requirement, and it is a way of looking at the issue that continues to have a large influence on political discussion (see, for example, President Bush's insistence that when there is a tax cut, everyone's taxes should be cut by roughly the same proportion).

From early on, there have also been dissenters from this approach, and at the present time, a number of the most prominent tax theorists reject it. Nevertheless, we will begin by explaining in detail what we think is wrong with an exclusive focus on the distribution of tax burdens, and why other political values must play a role in any adequate discussion of justice in taxation. This will also serve to distinguish our objections from those of other contemporary critics of the traditional approach.

There are also decisive objections to the traditional discussion of fairness even on its own terms. Still, an examination of those traditional ideas is an excellent way to bring out the nature and complexity of the issues of political morality that tax policy must address.[3] So we will start our discussion from inside the traditional framework.

II. Vertical Equity: The Distribution of Tax Burdens

Everyone agrees that taxation should treat taxpayers equitably, but they don't agree on what counts as equitable treatment. It is standard practice in addressing the question to distinguish between vertical and horizontal equity. According to this conception, vertical equity is what fairness demands in the tax treatment of people at different levels of income (or consumption, or whatever is the tax base), and horizontal equity is what fairness demands in the treatment of people at the same levels. Vertical equity is analytically more fundamental, since sameness of income takes on significance for policy purposes only if we believe that persons with different levels of income should be taxed differently.[4] Accordingly, we address vertical equity first.

As a limiting case, consider the simplest form of tax, which is a poll or head tax: each person pays the same dollar amount of tax, regardless of income. In addition to being simple, a head tax has a formal, if superficial, claim to being equitable, since it treats everyone literally the same. If this were fair, the question of vertical equity would be easily resolved—people with different incomes should not pay different amounts of tax, they should pay the same. But even the most virulent opponents of redistribution away from pretax incomes balk at the head tax; it is almost never defended as the appropriate form of a national income tax.[5]

Given the superficial equity of a scheme that takes the same amount of money from each person, why is a head tax almost universally regarded as obviously unjust? One answer is that there are relevant differences between taxpayers that make it fair to treat them differently—indeed, unfair to treat them the same.[6] This is where the topic of vertical equity begins—by asking what the relevant differences are between taxpayers that justify differential tax burdens.

We will review some traditional answers to this question. Our purpose, however, is to explain why the question itself is misguided. The injustice of the head tax has a more fundamental source.

It will be helpful to sketch in advance two main themes of our discussion. First, theories of vertical equity are frequently myopic, in that they attempt to treat justice in taxation as a separate and self-contained political issue. The result is not a partial account of justice in government, but rather a false one.[7] For what counts as justice in taxation cannot be determined without considering how government allocates its resources.

Myopia afflicts the contemporary legislative process in the United States in a simple and dramatic way, in the form of tables that set out the distribution of tax burdens associated with various tax reforms.[8] Most government transfers are excluded from these burden tables, including, most importantly, Social Security and Medicare payments.[9] This practice has been strongly criticized; as David Bradford writes, "economists have long recognized the essential equivalence between taxes and transfer payments."[10] It seems clear that a tax burden that is matched by an equivalent transfer is not, in the relevant sense, a burden at all.

But the problem would not be solved even if all money transfers were included in the burden tables. That too would be arbitrary, so long as we excluded in-kind benefits such as roads, schools, and police, not to mention the entire legal system that defines and protects everyone's property rights. If literally all government benefits were taken into account, however, we would notice that almost no one suffers a net burden from government. We would be forced to conclude that there is no separate issue of the fair distribution of tax burdens, distinct from the entirely general issue of whether government secures distributive justice.[11] This might be described as a question about the allocation of different *benefits* of taxation, expenditure, and other government policies to different individuals; but that looks very unlike the original question.

The only way to avoid this conclusion would be to assume some morally privileged hypothetical distribution of welfare or resources as the baseline against which to assess the burdens of government. And our second main objection to theories of vertical equity is that they commonly do just that. Implicit in those theories is a vision of government as a provider of services whose demands for payment intrude on a laissez-faire capitalist market economy that produces a presumptively legitimate distribution of property rights. Justice in taxation is then seen as the fair sharing out of tax burdens among individuals *as assessed from that baseline*.

The assumption that pretax market outcomes are presumptively just, and that tax justice is a question of what justifies *departures* from that baseline, appears to flow from an unreflective or "everyday" libertarianism about property rights. Though a consistent application of sophisticated libertarian political theory leads to deeply implausible results that hardly anyone actually accepts, in its naive, everyday version libertarianism is taken for granted in much tax policy analysis. We attempt a diagnosis of this situation in section VII, where we will present our most general theoretical objections to the tax burden approach.

Though our main aim is to explain that with the demand for a principle of vertical equity, the question has been wrongly posed from the start, in the following four sections we elaborate these criticisms of the idea of vertical equity by examining several traditional answers to the question—several views, that is, about which characteristics of taxpayers should be used to determine their differential tax burdens. Section III considers the principle that taxes should correspond to benefits received from government, and sections IV, V, and VI take up three interpretations of the principle that taxes should depend on ability to pay.

III. The Benefit Principle

One difference among taxpayers that certainly seems relevant is how much they benefit from government services. Many have thought that fairness in taxation requires that taxpayers contribute in proportion to the benefit they derive from government.[12] The implications of the benefit principle are usually said to be very unclear, on the ground that we lack even a roughly accurate measure of the benefits each individual receives from the government. But in fact, once we interpret the idea of benefits from government properly, the rough assessment of those benefits does not seem terribly problematic.

To come up with a measure or even an understanding of any kind of benefit (or burden) we need to ask, "Relative to what?"—we need to settle on a baseline. The magnitude of a benefit received is the difference between a person's baseline or prebenefit level of welfare and that person's level of welfare once the benefit has been conveyed. In this case, the baseline for determining the benefits of government is the welfare a person would enjoy if government were entirely absent; the benefit of government services must be understood as the difference between someone's level of welfare in a no-government world and their welfare with government in place.

What sort of life would be led in the total absence of government? It would be wrong to imagine life roughly as it is now, with jobs, banks, houses, and cars, and lacking only the most obvious government services such as Social Security, the National Endowment for the Arts, and the police. The no-government world is Hobbes's state of nature, which he aptly described as a war of all against all. And in such a state of affairs, there is little doubt that everyone's level of welfare would be very low and—importantly—roughly equal.[13] We cannot pretend that the differences in ability, personality, and inherited wealth that lead to great inequalities of welfare in an orderly market economy would have the same effect if there were no government to create and protect legal property rights and their value and to facilitate mutually beneficial exchanges. (We leave aside the fact that without government, the earth would sustain only a tiny fraction of its present human population, so that most of us wouldn't even exist in Hobbes's state of nature.)

If the relevant baseline for the assessment of benefit is the very low level of welfare, roughly the same for everyone, that people would have in the absence of government, then we can use people's actual levels of welfare, with government in place, as a rough measure of the benefit conveyed to them by government. And if income (somehow defined) were an acceptable measure of people's welfare, the benefit principle might seem to yield the following simple principle of vertical equity for an income tax: People should pay tax in proportion to their income, which is to say at the same percentage—a flat tax.[14]

Even leaving aside doubts about whether income is an acceptable measure of welfare, this conclusion does not follow. For the claim that justice is served by taxing in proportion to benefit must mean, not that each person should pay dollar amounts in proportion to benefits received, but rather that each person should be burdened, in real terms, in proportion to benefits received.[15] And once we take into account the familiar fact of the diminishing marginal utility of money, it is not at all clear what kind of rate structure for the income tax is recommended by the benefit principle. Depending on the way in which the marginal utility of money diminishes, the principle may recommend progressive, proportionate, or even regressive taxation.* The benefit principle would therefore be faced with a practical problem, even if it were ac-

---

*Taxation is progressive if the average rate increases with income (or whatever is the tax base), proportionate if the average rate remains constant as income increases, and regressive if the average rate decreases with income. (The term "progressive taxation" is sometimes used in a different sense in the tax policy literature, to refer to rising *marginal* rates.)

cepted as an ideal: Its implementation requires knowledge of how steeply marginal utility of income declines, and of how much the rate of decline varies from person to person.[16] That is a problem faced by many measures of vertical equity; we will return to it in a different context below.

But there is a more fundamental problem with the benefit principle: Whether or not it recommends proportional taxation, the benefit principle gives us no guidance on what the tax rate or rates should be, because it gives us no guidance as to the appropriate level of government expenditure. It takes expenditure as given, and allocates taxes in proportion to the resulting benefit. That is an example of what we mean by myopia.

At first glance, it is easy to overlook this problem. Shouldn't the rate be set at the level sufficient to pay for the government services that the democratic process deems desirable? Ordinary politics determines what government should provide; the benefit principle tells us how to fund government provision in a fair manner. But the trouble with this line of thought is that it pretends that the issue of the nature and extent of government services does not itself raise questions of justice. Once we acknowledge those questions, it is clear that the benefit principle cannot serve as a standard of tax justice.

The confusion is particularly apparent if we consider that on most accounts of social justice one of the aims of government is to provide (at least) minimal income support and health services to the otherwise indigent.[17] But if that is part of the aim of just government, it conflicts with the benefit principle. For though the very poor benefit less from government than the rich, they still benefit greatly as against the baseline of the war of all against all—especially in a country with at least a minimal welfare system. According to the benefit principle, then, the poor must pay for this benefit in proportion to its size. But it would be entirely pointless to provide minimal income support and then demand payment for the service.* The benefit principle is, in fact, incompatible,

---

*Noah Feldman has suggested that this absurdity could be avoided by a broader benefit principle understood not merely as a principle of tax policy but rather as a general principle of justice, according to which indi-

as a matter of political morality, with every account of social justice that requires government to provide any kind of income support or welfare provision whatsoever to the destitute (let alone more strongly egalitarian distributive aims).

Now there are accounts of social justice that reject all support for the destitute as illegitimate redistribution away from market returns. And so it might seem that the benefit principle is not myopic at all, but rather flows from a wider libertarian theory of political morality according to which the distribution of welfare produced by the market is presumptively just and should not be disturbed by government.

But the benefit principle is actually inconsistent with any such theory of justice. For if we assume that the pretax baseline is one of market outcomes undisturbed by government, and assume further that the resulting distribution is presumptively just, because people are entitled to what they get out of the market, then we will regard the benefit principle of taxation as unfair because it distorts that distribution. The benefit principle would have to take much more, in real terms, from those who do very well in the market than from those who do badly.[18] If market outcomes are presumptively just, that is unwarranted, and some other, less inequitable method must be found to pay for the costs of government and the legal protection of the market economy. We will examine such a standard—the principle of equal sacrifice—in section V below. The benefit principle, however, cannot be saved from incoherence by embedding it in a market-oriented theory of property rights. It is inconsistent with every significant theory of social and economic justice.

---

viduals are obligated to repay the benefits they receive from government not only through taxes, but by a combination of loyalty, legal obedience, and willingness to serve the state (by accepting conscription in wartime, for example). Then even those who receive income support from the state and pay no taxes would still be expected to repay their benefits in kind, so to speak. We will not attempt to evaluate this interesting proposal as a theory of distributive justice. In any event, it is not clear whether it could be worked out in a way that had definite implications for the allocation of tax burdens.

IV. Ability to Pay: Endowment

Historically, the main alternative to the benefit principle has been the principle that tax should be levied in accordance with taxpayers' "ability to pay." This is now the most commonly invoked criterion of vertical equity; in Germany, Italy, and Spain it has achieved constitutional status.[19]

On this view, what is inequitable about the head tax is that it ignores the fact that people differ in their ability to meet the burden of a tax payment. The notion of ability to pay is of course vague, and it has been interpreted in different ways. One initial ambiguity is this. Does it mean people's ability to pay tax by virtue of their actual economic situation—given the choices they have made and the income and wealth they now have? Or does it mean their ability to pay given the choices that they *could* make and the possibly higher income and wealth they therefore have the *ability* to earn? On the latter interpretation, the idea of ability to pay leads to the idea of *endowment taxation*: People should pay tax according to their endowment, which is defined as their ability to earn income and accumulate wealth. It is clear that potential income may be higher than actual income. Someone who abandons a successful business career to become an unsuccessful writer thenceforth earns below potential. Under an endowment tax, that person's tax bill would not decline along with income.

No one proposes the actual implementation of an endowment tax—the difficulty of measuring a person's maximum potential income is one obvious problem.* But among economists it is not unusual to employ the idea of taxation according to endowment as the fundamental principle of justification for tax policy. The thought is that an ideal or first-best taxation scheme would implement the endowment principle; actual proposed tax schemes are second best in that they aim toward the ideal but must deviate from it because of various practical considerations.[20]

---

*Another is the potential for interference with taxpayers' autonomy—see further chapter 5, sectionVIII.

The origin of the endowment principle lies in the earliest versions of the ability to pay approach. As originally understood, people's ability to pay tax, also called their "faculty," was understood to be a function of property or wealth.[21] This is natural enough—a person who has more wealth is in a literal sense able to transfer more money to the state. But in addition to ordinary property, people have what economists call "human capital": the resources of knowledge, ability, personality, connections, etc. that enable them to act productively—the most important case being the earning of wages in a market economy. So it is not surprising that by the nineteenth century some analysts began to suggest that the proper understanding of ability to pay was endowment in the full sense that includes a person's potential income.[22]

Since "liquidation" of human capital requires labor, however, the endowment interpretation of the idea of ability to pay has only an indirect relation to the value of fairness. It is one thing to believe that differences in actual income are relevant to the distribution of tax burdens because a higher-income person has more money available—and to believe that taxing everyone the same is unfair because people with more money should pay more. This simple and imprecise idea can hardly suffice as the basis for a theory of just taxation, as we shall see, but it certainly has initial intuitive plausibility. The same cannot be said for the very different idea that *potential* income should determine the distribution of tax burdens.

If two people, Bert and Kurt, earn the same amount, in fact, but Bert is earning at his full capacity and Kurt below his capacity, why might it be thought unfair to tax them the same absolute amount? We cannot say that Kurt has more money available, since he does not. Perhaps he has more leisure and is for that reason better off than Bert.[23] But this is not necessarily so: Perhaps Kurt and Bert work the same hours, but Kurt is earning less than he might because he has chosen to be a teacher rather than a lawyer.

But whether he takes it in the form of leisure or a lower-paying occupation, there is an advantage Kurt has over Bert, when it comes to the normal tax system: Something he cares about costs him income, but only income that he doesn't earn. So if taxes are levied only on actual income, Kurt will enjoy those advantages tax-free, so to speak. He won't be taxed on the income he forgoes by working less or by being a teacher rather than a lawyer—whereas Bert will be taxed on the income he has to earn to buy a BMW. This may seem an inequitable and arbitrary distinction. Equitable treatment might be thought to require that this difference be taken into account in the tax scheme, and that taxes not be assessed merely on cash earnings, in order to deny Kurt a free ride that he doesn't deserve.*

Equity is not, however, the main reason contemporary economists offer for endowment as the ideal principle of taxation. That case usually turns not on fairness or moral obligation[24] but rather on the fact that a tax on endowment, unlike a tax on actual income, attaches no disincentive to further labor.**

A tax on actual income has two kinds of behavioral influences that pull in opposite directions. The first is that it encourages people to choose more or more highly paid work; this is due to what economists call the income effect—taxes leave you poorer and thus reduce your opportunity to consume. The second, called the substitution effect, is that the tax encourages people to work less, by reducing the reward per unit of labor. Without the tax, an additional hour of work may be worth more than an hour of leisure; with the tax, the extra hour of work may be worth less than the hour of leisure. The tax on endowment or potential income, by contrast,

---

*Another reason why fairness might be thought to demand a higher absolute amount of tax from Kurt is that in falling short of his potential income he is in some sense evading his responsibilities. Walker (1888), making essentially this argument, concludes, about the likes of Kurt: "His social and industrial delinquency, so far from excusing him from any portion of his obligation, would, the rather, justify heavier burdens being laid upon him, in compensation for the injury which his ill example and evil behavior have inflicted upon the community" (15). Walker was the first president of the American Economic Association from 1885.

**We discuss justice-based arguments for an endowment tax in chapter five, section VIII.

is a lump-sum tax and therefore has only an income effect. There is no substitution effect because the same tax must be paid whether the additional hour is worked or not.

Why is a tax with no substitution effect preferable? The answer has nothing to do with fairness. Rather, it turns on an essentially utilitarian argument.[25] As a moral theory utilitarianism requires each person to do whatever it is that will best promote the aggregate welfare of everyone. But utilitarianism as applied to tax policy is not at all concerned with whether people do their duty, as such, and indeed gives no role whatsoever to considerations of individual moral responsibility. Instead, it focuses on institutional design as a way of affecting people's behavior.

The utilitarian has a purely instrumental interest in people's behavior. As applied to the problem of tax design, utilitarianism tells us that the best tax system is the one that is most effective in promoting aggregate welfare, through incentives and in other ways: The aim is to design a tax scheme that will encourage people to act in the way that will best serve this aggregate good. The substitution effect is always bad from that point of view, as it may lead a person not to work an extra hour who would otherwise choose to do so, thus discouraging a mutually beneficial exchange. So a lump-sum tax is ideal in terms of its effects on behavior. Of course, a head tax is a lump-sum tax as well, but it is easy to see why utilitarians would prefer an endowment tax: it gives more productive people greater incentives to work than less productive people. From a utilitarian point of view, leisure is better forgone by those who produce more for the price.[26] As has often been noted, utilitarianism is consistent with Marx's dictum from "The Critique of the Gotha Program": "from each according to his ability, to each according to his needs."

We can conclude that the standard economic case for embracing the endowment principle as the ideal principle of tax policy should not be understood as an interpretation of "ability to pay," since that phrase is meant to suggest an answer to the problem of vertical equity—the problem of determining what is a fair distribution of tax burdens among differently situated people. The standard justification is aggregate utility, not fairness.

V. Ability to Pay: Equal Sacrifice

We have seen that if the tax base is actual income, there is a straightforward sense in which it can seem equitable to ask for more tax from those who have more income: Those who have more money are better able to pay. Though it sounds plausible enough, this idea remains ambiguous. There are at least two different senses in which a richer person might be thought better able to pay than a poorer person. First, we might think that people with more money can afford to give away more in the sense that additional money is worth less to them in real terms, so they can pay more money than a poorer person—sometimes much more—with no greater loss in welfare. Alternatively, we might think that people with more money can afford to give away more because even if they sustain a larger real sacrifice they will be *left* with more: they will still have, in some sense, enough—and will still be better off than those who started out with less. John Stuart Mill took a clear stand in favor of the first of these possibilities; it is to him that we owe the influential principle of equal sacrifice.[27] (We return to the second possibility in the next section.)

According to the equal-sacrifice principle, a just tax scheme will discriminate among taxpayers according to their income, taking more from those who have more, so as to ensure that each taxpayer sustains the same loss of welfare—so that the real as opposed to monetary cost to each is the same. The key factual assumption here is again that of the diminishing marginal value of money; whether the equal-sacrifice principle leads to a proportional or a progressive tax scheme depends on the rate at which the marginal utility of income diminishes.

We do not know how steeply marginal utility declines, but the fact that the equal-sacrifice principle may require empirical speculation to implement does not show that it is incorrect. Rough guesswork will be a part of any plausible account of tax justice, and it is a serious mistake to prefer one account of justice to another *solely* because it seems easier to implement. As the economist Amartya Sen has said, "it is better to be roughly right than precisely wrong."

At this stage our question is the more fundamental one of whether the principle of equal sacrifice is plausible as a matter of political morality. A sacrifice is a burden; as with benefits, our understanding of the nature of a burden depends on the baseline we use for comparison. It is clear that the baseline envisaged for the principle of equal sacrifice is not the world without government and a war of all against all. That would be the right baseline if the principle concerned equality of *net* sacrifice—the burdens of government minus its benefits. However, as we know, government does not in fact impose a net sacrifice on anyone; assuming that we are talking only about governments that do not enslave, murder, or persecute parts of the population, each person is better off, post-tax, with government in place than without it. So equal net sacrifice relative to the miserable level of the no-government world is clearly not what advocates of the equal-sacrifice principle of tax fairness have in mind. Their idea has been that fair taxation will extract an equal sacrifice as measured against a baseline of pretax incomes, where those incomes are possible only in the presence of government.

Our principal objection to this approach is that it treats the justice of tax burdens as if it could be separated from the justice of the pattern of government expenditure—what we called earlier the problem of myopia. This is to treat "the collection of taxes as though it were only a common disaster—as though the tax money once collected were thrown into the sea."[28] In fact, taxes are imposed for a purpose, and an adequate criterion of justice in their imposition must take that purpose into account. What matters is not whether taxes—considered in themselves—are justly imposed, but rather whether the totality of government's treatment of its subjects, its expenditures along with its taxes, is just.

Taxes are not, in general, like criminal fines, which may be understood to impose symbolic or moral costs over and above their monetary costs. So understood, criminal fines *should* be fairly imposed considered in themselves, since improper fines harm or wrong a person even if they are easily "affordable," or are canceled out in financial terms by funds transferred from the state. There are, it is true, certain possible tax practices that are intrinsically unjust because of their discriminatory aims or effects; cash transfers would not adequately compensate the victims of this kind of tax injustice. But such exceptional cases—we discuss them in chapter 8—must not be taken as representative of our topic; as far as its purely economic impact is concerned, the justice of taxation is an issue that must be considered as part of the general subject of social justice.

Since taxation is not an entirely independent realm of justice, one cannot pronounce confidently that the state should extract an equal tax sacrifice from each person as measured against pretax incomes while remaining agnostic on the question of what a just expenditure policy would be. As Pigou wrote, more than fifty years ago:

> People's economic well-being depends on the whole system of law, including the laws of property, contract and bequest, and not merely upon the law about taxes. To hold that the law about taxes ought to affect different people's satisfactions equally, while allowing that the rest of the legal system may properly affect them very unequally, seems not a little arbitrary.[29]

However, the equal-sacrifice principle cannot be rejected as quickly as the benefit principle for, unlike the latter, it does make sense if embedded in a wider theory of justice that rejects all government expenditure or taxation to alter the distribution of welfare produced by the market. Such a libertarian theory of justice, typically based on either some notion of desert for the rewards of one's labor, or of strict moral entitlement to pretax market outcomes, limits the role of the state to the protection of those entitlements and other rights, along, perhaps, with the provision of some uncontroversial public goods. If (and only if) that is the theory of distributive justice we accept, the principle of equal sacrifice does make sense.

It makes sense because the theory limits government services to those that are needed to secure everyone's rights, in ways that can only be accomplished by state action. Paying for these minimal services that benefit everyone is then naturally understood as a matter of sharing out the cost of a common burden.

On this view, government should not be in the business of altering the distribution of welfare, but its services (police, roads, financial regulation, etc.) have to be paid for nevertheless. How should the burden be distributed? The equal-sacrifice principle would seem to provide the natural solution to this problem of fair taxation for a libertarian—what could be fairer, if we assume that the distribution of welfare produced by the market is just, than that everyone contribute the same amount in real (as opposed to monetary) terms?

As we saw, the benefit principle is less plausible from this perspective. By assessing everyone the same proportion of their total benefit from the existence of government, it exacts far more in real cost from the better-off and thus alters the presumptively just distribution produced by the free market. And the head tax could hardly be defended as a fair way to fund a government that is imposed on everyone, regardless of their wishes, since it hurts some people more than others and indeed hurts more those who are already worse off. Thus, the equal-sacrifice principle—taxing people differently so that everyone shares the same proportion of the common burden in real terms—has some initial claim to be taken seriously since there is *a* theory of justice in which it can be embedded.

However, it is important to emphasize that this approach cannot be generalized to other theories of justice. The separate treatment of justice in taxation as a sharing out of common burdens among the citizenry depends on the libertarian assumption that there is no comparable question of distributive justice in public expenditures or the provision of government services. If one rejects that assumption, the treatment of taxes as a "common disaster" has no further application.

An unreflective form of libertarianism casts a shadow over much discussion of tax policy; we will later discuss the severe damage this has done. For now we note that very few people are consciously committed to the libertarian theory of justice. Hardly anyone really believes that market outcomes are presumptively just and that justice does not require government to provide welfare support to those of its subjects who are destitute, without access to food, shelter, or health care. Thus, though the principle of equal sacrifice has been widely avowed over the past 150 years, the theory of justice it depends on has not been.

That dissonance at the level of first principles typically disappears at the level of concrete proposals for tax reform. When that stage is reached, the principle of equal sacrifice is in practice always abandoned: no one proposes a tax scheme that does not provide for a substantial personal exemption or tax-free level of income. And practically everyone supports some level of transfer payments to those who are genuinely unable to provide for themselves. Nevertheless, the dissonance at the level of first principles has important political consequences; we discuss it at length in section VII.

In the meantime, we must review some other interpretations of the general idea that taxes should be levied in accordance with ability to pay—interpretations that lack the radical implications of the equal-sacrifice principle.

VI. Ability to Pay as an Egalitarian Idea

As it has so far been understood, the principle of equal sacrifice requires that taxes impose the same real loss of welfare on each taxpayer. In the tax policy literature, this is sometimes referred to as the principle of equal *absolute* sacrifice, in order to contrast it with two other principles, those of equal proportional and equal marginal sacrifice.[30] The practice of presenting these three principles as interpretations of a common basic idea of equal sacrifice is misleading, as the latter two principles in fact have nothing to do with the idea that a fair tax scheme should impose the same sacrifice on everyone; rather, they are best understood precisely as rejections of that idea and its radical implications.

We need not here discuss the principle of equal marginal sacrifice, since it represents an essentially utilitarian approach and has nothing to do with the fair distribution of tax burdens.[31] The principle of equal proportional sacrifice, by contrast, is important in the current context, since it expresses an egalitarian interpretation of the idea of ability to pay. Even though this principle is rarely invoked explicitly any more, it corresponds to a very common way of thinking about tax fairness.

The principle of equal proportional sacrifice stipulates that individuals should sustain tax burdens in proportion to their level of welfare.[32] That means that the better off a person is, the greater the real sacrifice that should be exacted through taxation. The only thing equal about this pattern of taxation is the proportion of welfare each person loses. And an equal proportion, of course, is not an equal amount; if all give up the same proportion, the better-off give up more, in real terms (though they are also left with more). So the word "equal" is redundant in the label "equal proportional sacrifice"—"proportional sacrifice" denotes the same idea.

As we noted at the start of the previous section, one might interpret the idea of ability to pay not just in terms of the diminishing marginal utility of money, but rather as the political claim that better-off people can "afford" to sacrifice more, in real terms, than worse-off people, because they will still be left with more. This interpretation of the notion of ability to pay, which is required by the principle of proportional sacrifice, is dramatically at odds with the principle of equal sacrifice. The claim that those who are better off can afford a greater real sacrifice embraces taxation as a legitimate means of redistribution away from market outcomes, to the benefit of the worse-off at the expense of the better-off. The principle of proportional sacrifice thus rejects the libertarian theory of justice that implicitly lies behind the principle of equal sacrifice.

Since the underlying idea of the principle of proportional sacrifice must simply be that fair taxation will extract more, in real terms, from those who are better off, there should be no special magic in the formula of strict proportionality.[33] The same general idea could lead, for example, to the even more strongly egalitarian view that taxes should be levied at progressively *higher* proportions of real sacrifice as welfare rises.

That suggests what might seem to be an appealingly flexible way of thinking about tax justice: fair taxation imposes greater real burdens on those who are better off, but the exact rate of increase in the burdens is a matter to be settled by intuitive political judgment. Some such view—we could call it "the principle of increasing sacrifice"—is no doubt implicitly held by many people of an egalitarian disposition and draws them to favor progressive tax schemes.

Once again, however, this entire approach is flawed in its foundations. If the distribution produced by the market is not presumptively just, then the correct criteria of distributive justice will make no reference whatever to that distribution, even as a baseline. Distributive justice is not a matter of applying some equitable-seeming function to a morally arbitrary initial distribution of welfare. Despite what many people implicitly assume, the justice of a tax scheme cannot be evaluated simply by checking that average tax rates increase fast enough with income. Moreover, as we have seen, once we reject the assumption that the distribution of welfare produced by the market is just, we can no longer offer principles of tax fairness apart from broader principles of justice in government. If the distribution produced by the market is not presumptively just, then government should employ whatever overall package of taxation and expenditure policies best satisfies the correct criteria of justice; it is meaningless to insist that tax policy be fair in itself while ignoring the fairness of expenditures.

We can summarize this section and the previous one with two observations: (1) If the idea of taxation in accordance with ability to pay is made concrete through the principle of equal sacrifice, it depends on the radical view that the distribution of welfare produced by the market is presumptively just. (2) If, on the contrary, the idea of taxation in accordance with ability to pay is understood to mean that redistribution away from market returns is required by justice, then the goal of the vertical equity of taxation, considered apart from the justice of government expenditures, has been abandoned. And the vague idea of "ability to pay" will not help us when we move to the different question of what distributive aims a just government should have.

VII. The Problem of Everyday Libertarianism

We have said that the principle of equal sacrifice depends on the idea that the distribution of welfare produced by the market is presumptively just. That idea in turn implies that justice does not require a government to alleviate even the most serious inequalities that the market might produce, or to provide minimal subsistence for those who lack food, shelter, access to health care, or the means of buying those things.

Hardly anyone actually holds this radical view on distributive justice, but a muted version of it infects much everyday thinking about tax policy. Even those who believe that the principle of equal sacrifice is insufficiently egalitarian in its implications may persist with the notion that justice in taxation is a matter of securing a fair distribution of sacrifice as measured against a market-outcomes baseline. The mismatch between this way of thinking about tax policy and what people actually believe about distributive justice (let alone what it is most plausible to believe) is not just a harmless intellectual confusion. Unfortunately, it has great political significance.

Let us take a closer look at the market-oriented view of distributive justice required by the equal sacrifice approach. (The issues raised here are discussed in greater depth in the next chapter.) Libertarian views come in a variety of different forms, but the two that are most important for current purposes can be referred to as the rights-based and the desert-based.[34] The former turns on a commitment to strict moral property rights; it insists that each person has an inviolable moral right to the accumulation of property that results from genuinely free exchanges.

The implication for tax policy of rights-based libertarianism in its pure or absolute form is that no compulsory taxation is legitimate; if there is to be government, it must be funded by way of voluntary contractual arrangements.[35] On this extreme version of libertarianism we should never reach the issue of the fair distribution of mandatory tax burdens, because all such burdens are illegitimate. However, as explained in the previous section, a less absolute libertarian position would authorize compulsory taxation to support a government that permits the market to operate, and that would justify sharing out the burden equally.[36]

According to desert-based forms of libertarianism, on the other hand, the market gives people what they deserve by rewarding their productive contribution and value to others. Such a view would imply that the market-based distribution is presumptively just without raising any objection to compulsory taxation—provided, again, that the burden is shared out equally.

We discuss desert-based theories of justice in chapters 3 and 5. Here we note just one point. The notion of desert entails that of responsibility; we cannot be said to deserve outcomes for which we are not in any way responsible. Thus, to the extent that market outcomes are determined by genetic or medical or social luck (including inheritance), they are not, on anyone's account, morally deserved. Since nobody denies that these kinds of luck at least partly determine how well a person fares in a capitalist economy, a simple and unqualified desert-based libertarianism can be rejected out of hand.

Both forms of libertarianism have implausibly radical consequences. But there is a still more fundamental problem with this approach to tax justice—a conceptual problem. Our use of libertarianism to make sense of the equal-sacrifice principle has relied so far on the following assumption: That so long as government does not pursue redistributive expenditure policies, the pretax distribution of resources can be regarded as the distribution produced by a free market. But, in fact, this is deeply incoherent.

There is no market without government and no government without taxes; and what type of market there is depends on laws and policy decisions that government must make. In the absence of a legal system supported by taxes, there couldn't be money, banks, corporations, stock exchanges, patents, or a modern market economy—none of the institutions that make possible the existence of almost all contemporary forms of income and wealth.

It is therefore logically impossible that people should have any kind of entitlement to all their pretax income. All they can be entitled to is what they would be left with after taxes under a legitimate system, supported by legitimate taxation— and this shows that we cannot evaluate the legitimacy of taxes by reference to pretax income. Instead, we have to evaluate the legitimacy of after-tax income by reference to the legitimacy of the political and economic system that generates it, including the taxes which are an essential part of that system. The logical order of priority between taxes and property rights is the reverse of that assumed by libertarianism.

This problem could not be avoided by moving from a baseline of actual pretax incomes to a hypothetical baseline of incomes in a government-free market world. There is no natural or ideal market. There are many different kinds of market system, all equally free, and the choice among them will turn on a range of independent policy judgments.

A flourishing capitalist economy requires not only the enforcement of criminal, contract, corporate, property, and tort law. (Those laws themselves are not natural but include evolving and contested accounts of limited liability, bankruptcy, enforceability of agreements, contract and tort remedies, etc.) In addition, most economists assume, it requires at a minimum a regime of anti-trust legislation to promote competition, and control over interest rates and the money supply to alternately stimulate or retard economic growth and control inflation. Then there are such matters as transport policy, regulation of the airwaves, and the way government alleviates so-called negative externalities of the market, such as environmental degradation.

All these functions of government are taken for granted by even the most ardent market enthusiasts. The problem for the sacrifice view here is that the choices government makes in discharging these functions affect market returns. How much profit an iron-ore smelter can generate will depend on the prevailing regime of environmental law. A person's fortunes on the bond market depend on government-influenced interest rate fluctuations. The upshot is that even if the destitute are left to fend for themselves, it still cannot be said that pretax outcomes are simply market outcomes. They are, instead, the returns generated by a market regulated in accordance with a certain set of government policies.

Choices about these matters cannot be made without appeal to substantive social values that go beyond whatever internal logic there is to the idea of a competitive market. Since that is so, the idea of a politically neutral market world that can serve as the baseline required by the sacrifice approach to taxation is a fantasy. Any pretax distribution—real or imaginary—is already shaped in part by judgments of political morality, and it is impossible to address questions of tax fairness without evaluating those judgments.

Altogether, the case against using pretax outcomes as the baseline against which fairness in the distribution of tax burdens can be assessed is so strong as to make it puzzling how anyone could have been attracted to this way of thinking about tax justice. The answer lies in the enormous appeal of what we have called everyday libertarianism. Even though the two ideas of strict, unqualified moral property rights and desert in market rewards may not survive cursory critical reflection, they are hard to banish from our everyday thinking. In both cases, we believe, the illusion is supported by the illegitimate extension of more restricted concepts beyond the boundaries within which they actually apply.

Consider first the idea of moral property rights in pretax income. We all know that people have full *legal* right to their *net* (post-tax) income; subject to contractual or family obligations, their money is legally theirs to do with as they wish. A legal property right to net income is obviously not an absolute moral property right to anything (let alone to pretax market returns), but in daily life it is hard to prevent the strong sense of legal rights from sliding into a sense of a much more fundamental right or entitlement.

From this point of view, it isn't just that it makes good pragmatic or economic sense for government to protect our current legal entitlements; it isn't even that, having once created these legal rights, government is morally required to protect the legitimate expectations that those rights generate. At the everyday level of what it feels like to live and work in a capitalist economy, the sense of entitlement to net income is firmer than that—we are inclined to feel that what we have earned belongs to us without qualification, in the strong sense that what happens to that money is morally speaking *entirely* a matter of our say-so. Though everyone knows that even our right to spend the money in our pockets is circumscribed, for example, by the obligation to pay applicable sales taxes, the instinctive sense of unqualified ownership has remarkable tenacity.

If people intuitively feel that they are in an absolute sense morally entitled to their net incomes, it is not surprising that politicians can get away with describing tax increases (which diminish net income) as taking from the people what belongs to them. It is then a short step to the thought that tax cuts give us back "our money"* and indeed that all taxation takes what belongs to us; what we are fundamentally entitled to is our *pretax* incomes.

Of course, virtually no one really believes that all taxation is illegitimate because it takes what belongs to us without our consent. Everyday libertarianism is, as we have said, a muted or confused version of the real thing. Nevertheless, the confused idea that net income is what we are left with after the government has taken away some of what *really* belongs to us certainly helps explain the conviction that the pretax distribution of material welfare is presumptively just (how could a distribution that gives people precisely what they are morally entitled to be unjust?), and that the question of justice in taxation is therefore properly a question of determining what is a fair distribution of sacrifice as assessed from that baseline.

We can comment more briefly on the other powerful influence, the idea of desert. Market returns are to a certain extent affected by a person's effort and willingness to take risks. Since that is so, it can seem preposterous to those who are both better-off and very hard-working to suggest that they do not deserve to be paid more than others who may be lazy and unadventurous. And, perhaps because people care more about what unjustly harms them than about what unjustly benefits them, they can easily ignore the fact that some of the other factors contributing to their economic success are not in any sense their responsibility and therefore can be said to

---

*As George W. Bush has often said of the federal budget surplus: "The surplus doesn't belong to the government, it belongs to the people."

have produced advantages that are not deserved. The natural idea that people deserve to be rewarded for thrift and industry slides into the much broader notion that all of pretax income can be regarded as a reward for those virtues. Here too, a normative concept is being taken beyond the context in which it legitimately applies.

So the unreflective ideas that we have unqualified moral entitlement to what we earn in the market and that higher market returns are in some sense deserved as a reward arise naturally within the everyday outlook of participants in a capitalist economy. It is true that almost nobody follows through on the idea that a market-generated distribution of welfare is intrinsically just—nearly everyone accepts the need for *some* kind of public assistance to the destitute, and not even the most radically antiegalitarian politicians argue for a tax scheme without a significant personal exemption. Nonetheless, everyday libertarianism has a distorting effect, for these exceptions to the libertarian outlook tend to be regarded as charitable gestures that do not challenge the basic approach to distributive justice. By placing the burden of proof on departures from market outcomes, everyday libertarianism skews the public debate about tax policy and distributive justice.

Tax policy analysis needs to be emancipated from everyday libertarianism; it is an unexamined and generally nonexplicit assumption that does not bear examination, and it should be replaced by the conception of property rights as depending on the legal system that defines them. Since that system includes taxes as an absolutely essential part, the idea of a prima facie property right in one's pretax income—an income that could not exist without a tax-supported government—is meaningless. There is no reality, except as a bookkeeping figure, to the pretax income that each of us initially "has," which the government must be equitable in taking from us. It isn't that there are no questions of equity here—justice is central to the design of property rights—only that this is the wrong way to pose them.

The tax system is not like an assessment of members of a department to buy a wedding gift for a colleague. It is not an incursion on a distribution of property holdings that is already presumptively legitimate. Rather, it is among the conditions that *create* a set of property holdings, whose legitimacy can be assessed only by evaluating the justice of the whole system, taxes included. Against such a background people certainly have a legitimate claim on the income they realize through the usual methods of work, investment, and gift—but the tax system is an essential part of the background which creates the legitimate expectations that arise from employment contracts and other economic transactions, not something that cuts in afterward.

There is no default answer to the question of what property system is right—no presumptively just method of distribution, deviations from which require special justification. The market has many virtues, but it does not relieve us of the task of coming to terms with the real values at stake in tax policy and the theory of distributive justice. There are no obvious answers to the range of questions about distributive justice we will pose in the next chapter; but one thing that should be obvious is that those questions must be faced by tax theory.

VIII. Horizontal Equity

Whereas the label "vertical equity" refers to a normative question, the label "horizontal equity" states a normative conclusion: People with the same incomes (or other relevant economic measure) should pay the same amount of tax. However, these two dimensions of tax equity are not really distinct. Horizontal equity is just a logical implication of any traditional answer to the question of vertical equity. If tax justice is fully captured by a criterion that directs government to tax each level of income at a certain rate, it simply follows that people with the same pretax incomes should be taxed at the same rate.

The reason so much attention has been devoted to issues of horizontal equity by tax theorists is that there are many apparent violations of the norm of equal tax from equal income in most actual tax regimes, and many possible violations that are not apparent, but need to be rooted out. A central question in this literature has been whether apparent violations of horizontal equity show themselves as true violations once the issue of tax incidence has been properly taken into account.

To take a standard example, the preferential tax treatment of state and municipal bonds in the United States is not regarded as a violation of horizontal equity, since the bond market adjusts by bidding up the price of the tax-exempt bonds. As a result, there is no inequity at the level of tax-paying purchasers of bonds (but rather instead a question about why state and local governments should receive this economic benefit courtesy of the tax code).[37] In other cases of apparent horizontal inequities, however, the issue of incidence is not so easy to determine.

A further reason for scholarly attention to horizontal equity is that it is a controversial question in economics just what the appropriate operational measure of degrees of horizontal equity might be. As Alan Auerbach and Kevin Hassett write: "From Musgrave . . . on, there is general agreement that horizontal equity is important, but little agreement on quite what it is."[38]

But if what we have said about the traditional criteria of vertical equity is right, there is a fundamental objection to the traditional concern with horizontal equity as well. For we have argued precisely that tax justice cannot be fully captured by a criterion that simply directs government to tax certain incomes at certain rates (based on some principle of sacrifice or benefit). Tax justice must be part of an overall theory of social justice and of the legitimate aims of government. Since that is so, there can be no blanket rule that persons with the same pretax income or level of welfare must pay the same tax.[39] The strong pull of such a rule seems again to be due to everyday libertarianism; if we assume that the pretax distribution provides the moral baseline from which taxation must begin, it is natural to think that it would be unjust for people with the same incomes or welfare not to pay the same amount in tax.

Once we abandon the presumption of the moral significance of the pretax world, we see that differential treatment of people with the same income may or may not be warranted depending on our overall theory of justice. If it is a legitimate social goal to encourage home ownership, for example, by exempting imputed income from owner-occupied housing and allowing a deduction for mortgage interest payments, and if this practice is innocent from the point of view of distributive justice (both contestable premises), then the unequal treatment of buyers and renters raises no further issue of justice.

That is not to say, however, that anything goes in tax policy. Some forms of discrimination among taxpayers will count as unjust even if they do serve other legitimate goals. The familiar suspect categories of race, sex, sexuality, and religion come to mind. But a ban on invidious discrimination through the tax system is not the same as a blanket ban on taxing differently those who earn the same. We discuss the topic of tax discrimination in detail in chapter 8.

3

Economic Justice in Political Theory

I. Political Legitimacy

In the present chapter, we describe the issues in moral and political theory that bear most directly on the evaluation of tax policy. This will involve a survey of contemporary views about the justification and criticism of political and social institutions.

In this section and the next, we introduce some concepts that provide the general framework for such moral assessments. Sections III and IV distinguish between two important ways taxes can be used by the government to benefit its citizens. Sections V, VI, and VII take up the issue of distributive justice, considering different answers to the question of how costs and benefits should be allocated among many individuals when their interests conflict, and the relation of justice to equality and inequality. Sections VIII and IX consider the ways in which values of freedom and individual responsibility can be embodied in a social and economic system. Sections X and XI discuss different attitudes toward the market economy; and section XII takes up the problem of whether political values and private economic motives can combine to sustain a morally coherent social order.

The framework for the entire discussion is the question of the appropriate relation of the individual to the collectivity, through the institutions of the state.* A state has a near-monopoly of force within its territory, and it has the authority to coerce individuals to comply with decisions arrived at by some nonunanimous collective choice procedure. What are the legitimate aims for which such power may be used, and what, if anything, limits the way it may legitimately be exercised over individuals?

These are questions about what we may be said to owe to our fellow citizens, and what kind of sovereignty we should retain over ourselves, free from the authority of the state, even when we are members of it and subject to its control in certain respects. Those questions define the issue of political legitimacy. What, then, are the legitimate ends of government, and what are the legitimate means of pursuing those ends, particularly insofar as they involve the taxing power?

It is essential to keep in mind, when considering these questions, that government doesn't only *regulate* people's lives. By providing the institutional conditions without which modern civilization and economic activity could not exist, government is substantially responsible for the kinds of lives that people can lead. The issue of political legitimacy therefore applies to this framework itself and to the kinds of options, choices, and lives it makes possible, as well as to the government's control over the conduct of individuals within the framework.

That means that when we ask what we owe our fellow citizens, by way of positive assistance or mutual restraint, it cannot be understood as a question addressed to us as prepolitical beings, who will use the state as an instrument

---

*There is also a field of international political theory, involving ideas about global justice and even international taxation, but we will leave all such questions aside. As things are now, taxation is an issue for nation-states and their subdivisions, even if political developments and considerations of justice will lead eventually to the development of supranational structures with the power to tax individuals. The European Community, for example, is supported by contributions from member states, not by direct taxes on their citizens.

to fulfill our interpersonal obligations. The situation is rather that we begin from the point of view of members of an existing society—beings formed by a civilization and leading lives that would be inconceivable without it—and our task is to decide what norms the design and regulation of that social structure should respect, as an expression of the consideration that is due from each of us to our fellow members as well as the independence we are entitled to retain from one another.

Taxes are part of that structure, but they have to be evaluated not only as legal demands by the state on individuals but also as contributions to the framework within which all those individuals live. Ultimately, the question of political legitimacy is the question of what kind of framework we can all find it morally acceptable to live inside of, and it is to that question that values such as liberty, responsibility, equality, efficiency, and welfare have to be applied.

II. Consequentialism and Deontology

A fundamental division runs through these debates, between two types of normative theory—those that focus on outcomes, conventionally called "consequentialist," and those that focus on actions, conventionally called "deontological" (from the Greek word meaning "ought"). Consequentialist theories of justification hold that the ultimate standard for evaluating a policy or institution lies in the value of its overall consequences—the benefits minus the costs, for all those affected. Deontological theories hold that there are other standards, independent of overall consequences, which determine how a government may or may not treat people. Those standards identify individual rights, requirements of fairness or equal treatment, prohibitions against arbitrary discrimination, and so forth, and prescribe what should and should not be done in a way that is at least partly independent of the consequences. There is further variation and disagreement within each of these two categories, and there are also theories that combine elements of both kinds. But this rough division in attitudes to the nature of ultimate justification is an important one.

Since it is a disagreement at the level of theory, it does not inevitably result in disagreements at the level of policy. Both consequentialists and deontologists will have no difficulty explaining why murder should be against the law. A consequentialist can say that the benefits in safety and security are well worth the costs in enforcement, and a deontologist can say that one of the legitimate uses of state power is to protect individuals against violation of their right to life.

In fact, consequentialist theories usually accept the existence of rights, but they deny that rights are morally fundamental. Rather, they hold that rights must be justified by the overall benefits of a system that recognizes them. On this view rights, and other requirements of the kind thought fundamental by deontologists, have to be derived from something still more fundamental and are valid only insofar as they can be justified consequentially.

We can illustrate this by considering the difference between two explanations of property rights—the moral category most directly relevant to tax policy. All except the most radically utopian moral and political theories recognize the legitimacy of property rights and the importance of their definition and protection by a just society. But deontological theories, deriving from the tradition of Locke, hold that property rights are in part determined by our individual sovereignty over ourselves, including the fundamental right to the free exercise of our individual abilities and efforts, the right to cooperate freely with others for mutual benefit, and the right to dispose freely of what we have legitimately acquired.[1] Property rights, on this view, are substantially shaped by a right of individual freedom that does not need a consequentialist justification.

Consequentialist theories, on the other hand, deriving from the tradition of Hume, hold that property rights are justified by the larger social utility of a set of fairly strict conventions and laws protecting the security of property.[2] Only in a society in which such rights are recognized, and theft is prohibited and contracts and wills enforced, can there be the sort of economic cooperation, long-term planning, and capital accumulation that make economic growth and prosperity possible. Without a system of property rights, we would be in Hobbes's state of nature, rather than in a civilized and technologically advanced society. According to the consequentialist approach, the evaluation of alternative systems of property rights depends entirely on which system best promotes the general welfare or some other collective good that is taken to be the aim of social organization. Property rights are not, on this view, in any sense natural or pre-institutionally inherent in the individual: rather, they are the consequence of laws, rules, and conventions designed to promote other values, such as prosperity and secure expectations.

Since taxes are essentially modifications of property rights that entitle the state to control over part of the resources generated by the economic life of its citizens, the evaluation of taxes will be much affected by whether one adopts a deontological or a consequentialist conception. Essentially, the difference is this: On a deontological approach, there is likely to be a presumption of some form of natural entitlement that determines what is yours or mine and what isn't, and this prima facie presumption has to be overridden by other considerations if appropriation by taxes is to be justified. On a consequentialist approach, by contrast, the tax system is simply part of the design of any sophisticated modern system of property rights. There is no prima facie presumption against taxation because there is no preinstitutional conception of what is "my" property. Everything is conventional. Any system has to be evaluated by comparison with alternative designs (involving different taxes or even public ownership in some sectors), entirely by reference to its effectiveness in promoting desirable social and economic results.

While this distinction between deontological and consequentialist approaches may become blurred somewhat in the discussion that follows, it ought to be kept in mind as a rough division between types of justification and criticism.[3] It will show up in our discussion of both the legitimate ends of governmental action and the legitimate means of pursuing those ends. If property rights are entirely conventional and taxes are merely part of the legal means of defining their boundaries, then the assessment of tax policy will take a rather different form from what would be appropriate if property rights have a natural basis in individual liberty and inviolability.

We would also like to mention a third type of view, which can be described as deontological, though it is very different from the Lockean conception. This is Hegel's theory that individuals have a right to possess some minimal amount of property in order to express their freedom by embodying their will in external objects.[4] It is a more positive conception of the right to property than Locke's theory, which is mainly negative because it depends on freedom from interference in the acquisition and use of property.

The Hegelian view has less prominence in contemporary political debate, but its spirit may have been assimilated by some consequentialist positions, which favor a social minimum as a positive right. At any rate, it seems important to us because it identifies a basic core of purely personal property rights that are essential for individual liberty, but that do not support the broader general presumption against state interference with private property that has often been derived from the Lockean conception of natural property rights. The sphere of morally required individual discretion over one's personal property does not extend far enough, in the Hegelian conception, to imply anything about the tax structure.

Our own view, as will emerge, is that property rights are conventional, but that there is room in their design and justification for the consideration of other rights and deontological values that are more fundamental, as well as consequentialist values. While the protection of some form of private property is an essential part of human freedom, the overall structure of the system of property rights should be determined largely on other grounds.

III. Public Goods

Turning now to a more systematic examination of the range of values that bear on the legitimacy of political institutions, we will have to divide the discussion into a number of components. Let us start with the broad division between ends and means, and consider first ends. The ends that may be claimed as legitimate for the state and that affect tax policy can be ranged under three headings: public goods, benefits to individuals, and distributive justice.

Public goods are the least controversial, since they include the minimal conditions considered necessary in any theory of government for all the other advantages of civilization: domestic peace and security, some kind of legal system, and protection against foreign invasion. Public goods are defined as those that cannot be provided to anybody unless they are provided to everybody. If violent crime, environmental pollution, the threat of fire, or communicable diseases are kept under control in a territory, then everyone living in that territory automatically benefits, and no one can be excluded. If one tried to support such goods by private subvention, there would be no way of excluding free riders, who would enjoy the good without paying—at least no way short of exile. The obvious way of getting everyone to pay their share is through taxation, coercively imposed.

The provision of public goods as an end places the least strain on conditions of political legitimacy, because it does not require any assumptions about how much, as fellow citizens, we should care about one another. It assumes only that we care about ourselves. Each individual has a direct personal interest in the maintenance of these desirable conditions and cannot enjoy them unless they are provided in a way that makes them available to others. So the motivation behind such provision is the minimal one of collective self-interest—a convergence of individual interests on a common end—though different issues will arise when it comes to sharing out the cost.

There is room for argument about what should be included among the public goods that simply must be provided by the state. In addition to public goods in the strict sense—those from which no one can be excluded—there are other institutions that clearly confer a public benefit, so that their provision by the state is supported by the motive of collective self-interest. Roads, air traffic control, a postal system, some regulation of the airwaves depending on the technological situation, education that ensures near-universal literacy, the maintenance of public health, a reliable system of civil law—all these are plausible candidates for systemic conditions that have benefits for everyone in the society through their large effects on safety, the economy, and the smooth functioning of social institutions. Some might wish to include among the public goods the prevention of abject poverty, as a condition of social peace. Others might say that the preservation of natural wilderness, or historic architecture, or the support of the performing and creative arts and of museums, should count partly as public goods, since their existence contributes to the pride that all citizens can take in their country. These examples seem to combine advantage to particular individuals (e.g., subsidized musicians and those who go to their concerts) with a more general public benefit (a national cultural identity, in this case).

At any rate, if one adds some of these further collective goods to the basic core of defense and the maintenance of law and order, the costs can be considerable. And that leads to the more controversial question of how those costs should be allocated among citizens all of whom benefit from the goods but whose resources differ. Should there be some effort to make contribution proportional to the quantity of benefit, or should it be proportional to resources, or should it be the same for everyone?

But this way of putting the question is too simple, because it presupposes an antecedent distribution of bundles of resources, prior to the provision of public goods, and as we have emphasized in chapter 2, there is no such thing. The real question is one of deciding among alternative systems of public provision financed through taxation, by comparing their different and disparate consequences for the lives of the individuals living under them, including the resources they are left with after taxes. The language of allocation of costs is just a simplified and potentially misleading way of talking about this comparison among systems of public finance. Here we have moved over to questions about means rather than ends and also to the topic of distributive justice as an end.

There is also the issue of the grounds on which it is to be decided *how much* of these public goods the society should want. Since they are paid for through taxes which divert some of the gross national product from private use, some method is needed to evaluate the competing claims of these alternative employments of resources. Is that marginal dollar better spent at the discretion of a private individual or on an improved highway system or supersonic bomber? We shall return to this question in chapter 4.

IV. Benefits for Individuals

The next topic is the large one of state action that aims to benefit individuals, not by means of a public good that can only be supplied for everyone at once, but rather by providing certain advantages to individuals one by one. Those advantages may be made available to everyone, but that is not a condition of their possibility, as with public goods.

Included prominently in this category are social services such as unemployment compensation, disability benefits, retirement pensions, child care support, health care, aid to dependent children, food stamps, free school lunches, and so forth. Also included are many kinds of educational support, including public universities, subsidized student loans, publicly financed scholarships, and financial support, direct and indirect (through tax deductions, for example), to private institutions.

Most straightforwardly, some individuals can be benefited through the tax system by being less heavily taxed than others, while receiving benefits that are supported by the taxes of everyone. One form such advantage can take is the exemption from tax of all income below a certain level. Another form is deductibility or exclusion from the tax base of certain expenditures or forms of income. Another is tax credits for certain types of expenditure, or measures like the earned income tax credit, which amounts to a negative income tax for low earners. And, of course, differences in the rate structure itself have a large effect. All these measures leave some individuals with more resources at their private disposal than they would have if the distribution of taxes were different, and others with less.

But if we are interested in the effects of government policies on the welfare of individuals, then the direct provision of benefits, either through public provision or through tax relief, is only part of the story. People are benefited and harmed in all kinds of ways that are not the direct result of government action, but that may still be affected by government policies: The effects of fiscal policy on private employment, productivity, growth, savings, and investment, and thereby on everyone's standard of living, are just as important in considerations of individual welfare as what the government does directly.

This means that the relevant considerations, from a moral point of view, have to be taken broadly, in a way that does not distinguish between direct and indirect benefit. The normative question about the appropriate ends of government, at this point, is whether they include the promotion of people's welfare, or some aspects of their welfare, and the prevention of individual misfortune. Should government policies, as part of their rationale, be designed with the aim of eliminating poverty, curing illness, raising the average or minimum standard of living, increasing people's lifespans, and making them happier? Or are these aims that people can be presumed to have for themselves individually, but that they should not take on as a collective responsibility, and in particular should not impose on others through government coercion which forces some citizens to contribute through their taxes to the welfare of others (or to put it more neutrally: leaves some citizens with fewer after-tax resources so that others may be better off)?

We see here a contrast with the rationale for state provision of public goods, which benefit everyone and in which everyone therefore has a direct personal interest. A conception of the state as an instrument for the pursuit of collective self-interest would include among its aims the provision of those public goods that are worth their cost in forgone private expenditures. This conception of the state is due to Hobbes, who thought that sovereign power was justified to enforce those conditions on our relations to one another (such as the rules of property) that it was in everyone's interest to make sure that everyone would adhere to, but that would not be maintained unless they were coercively enforced, because it was in no one's interest to adhere to them individually.[5]

By contrast, considerations of the general welfare have to appeal to something more than each individual's self-interest. If, through the agency of the state, we are to think of ourselves as aiming at everyone's benefit and not just our own, the reason for this must be that other people's welfare is a good that we have reason to care about, at least in the context of political choice.

This opens up the further large topic of the right way to interpret the idea of welfare or benefit for a collection of individuals, each of whom may be affected differently by any given policy.

V. Efficiency and Utilitarianism

The least adventurous conception of benefit to a number of individuals is the conception of Pareto optimality, also often called efficiency. One situation, A, is a Pareto improvement over another, B, or is said to be Pareto superior to it, if at least one person is better off in A than in B, and no one is worse off. Clearly, no one could object to the move from B to A, except perhaps on grounds of fairness ("Why not me?"). Clearly, Pareto improvement is one species of improvement in the general welfare. A situation is Pareto optimal, or efficient, if there is no way of moving to a situation that would be Pareto superior to it—no way of making anybody better off without making somebody else worse off.

The trouble is that this conception is of little use in evaluating government policies. Inefficiency is, of course, something to be avoided; but in real life, for almost any two policies that can be compared in their effects on individuals, each will be better for some people and worse for others. Neither will be Pareto superior to the other. A generous child care policy will benefit families with children by comparison to families without; a different policy will do the reverse; almost any change in the tax code will help some and hurt others; and so on.

If efficiency were the only standard, there would be no way to choose between two policies neither of which was at least as good for everybody as the other. For this reason, moral and political theorists generally use richer conceptions of the general welfare, conceptions that permit advantages and disadvantages to different individuals to be combined in the assessment of an overall outcome and in the comparison of alternatives.[6] These conceptions are true theories of social justice, because they govern the design of social systems in virtue of their overall effects on the lives of their members, beyond the requirement of efficiency.

The simplest and best-known theory of this kind is utilitarianism.[7] Utilitarianism takes the happiness or welfare of individuals as the basic currency of moral evaluation and assesses outcomes by subtracting the overall costs from the overall benefits, measured in these terms. Utilitarianism holds that one should try to maximize the total happiness of the members of a society in designing its policies and institutions. This is a standard of radical impartiality: it says that everyone's happiness counts equally, and that in our role as members of a society concerned with the justice of its institutions, we should care as much about the welfare of everyone else as about our own.

It doesn't mean that each official act should aim at increasing the general welfare, since some of the most useful institutions for promoting the general welfare, such as property rights and the legal system, depend on adhering to certain rules, without considering the general welfare in each case. But the ultimate standard, whether acts, laws, conventions, or policies are being evaluated, is the overall effect on people's happiness or welfare. This is, therefore, a consequentialist theory.

Utilitarianism requires some measure of utility that allows one to compare, add, and subtract effects on different people—a *metric*, as it is called, for what counts as good or bad for individuals, and how much. In fact, not only utilitarianism but all political theories with a consequentialist element—theories that evaluate policies and institutions in part by their beneficial and harmful effects on individuals—require some kind of metric to be able to compare the outcomes of different policies. One needs a common currency to add up what is good or bad for people, in order to be able to compare the great range of social effects on different individuals with their different tastes and values.

There is controversy over the choice of metric. It is a normative or moral controversy, because it is about what should count, in the lives of individuals, when we are deciding what collective policies a government should follow toward them. One question is whether the metric should have a subjective basis—such as the satisfaction or frustration of each individual's desires and preferences, whatever they are—or whether it should have an objective basis, for example, a list of familiar goods and evils like health and illness, longevity and early death, wealth and poverty, knowledge and ignorance, friendship and loneliness, and so forth. If, without being able to define it, we accept the social goal of maximizing the general welfare, then these issues of measurement are important for the application of a utilitarian standard.

But, more generally, the choice of a metric is an important question for any theory that is consequentialist, even in part—that requires us to compare the value of alternative outcomes. In the context of political theory and the legitimate aims of fiscal policy, the metric will determine the kinds of benefits and protections that it is incumbent on a society to promote for its members. Should we care about one another's subjective satisfaction, or only about certain more basic or concrete benefits? And should benefits of all kinds be included, or should social responsibility be concerned primarily with protecting people against objective harms and securing their vital needs?[8]

Apart from its use of experiential happiness as a metric, classical utilitarianism is distinguished from other theories of justice by two conspicuous and controversial features: its acceptance of aggregation and its indifference to distribution. By aggregation is meant the adding up of benefits and disadvantages from the lives of different individuals to make up a total, for the purpose of utilitarian evaluation of outcomes. It means, in particular, that a total utility made up of small advantages for each of a sufficiently large number of individuals can outweigh a large disutility, consisting of a major sacrifice for a small number of individuals.

Indifference to distribution means that utilitarianism ranks outcomes solely by reference to total benefits minus total costs, without any preference for a more rather than less equal spread of those benefits and costs among individuals. Utilitarianism would prefer a higher total of happiness to a lower total, even if the higher total involved a great range, with some people blissful and others miserable, while the lower total was the result of everyone's falling into a more moderate range.

These features have led critics to object that utilitarianism does not take seriously the distinction between persons.[9] The objection is that even though aggregation and maximization of total happiness make sense in the decisions of an individual faced with the choice whether to make sacrifices in the expectation of later rewards in the course of a single life, the kinds of trade-offs of costs in exchange for benefits that are acceptable in that context are not acceptable when the trade-offs are made across the lives of different individuals, as is the case in situations of social choice. Sacrificing one person for another is not like sacrificing my present comfort for my future prosperity.

These doubts have led to the development of alternative theories that incorporate distributional values in the assessment and comparison of socioeconomic systems. Such values usually include some bias in favor of equality, or at least toward the reduction of certain forms of inequality, in the distribution of either subjective welfare or objective resources.

VI. Distributive Justice, Fairness, and Priority to the Worst Off

The simplest form of such preference is what has been called the *pure priority view*, which counts an improvement to the welfare of someone worse off more heavily than an improvement of the same absolute magnitude to the welfare of someone better off.[10] This could be combined with a standard of maximizing the total, calculated in this new way, with the implication that the preference for improvements to the worse off can sometimes be outweighed by sufficiently greater improvements, or improvements for sufficiently greater numbers, among the better off.

A more radically egalitarian view would give strict priority to improvements in the condition of the worst off. This is the position that John Rawls calls the *difference principle*, according to which differences in wealth and standard of living between different social groups are justified only to the extent that the system that generates those inequalities also does at least as well for the interests of the worst-off group as any alternative system.[11] Such a standard, by contrast with a maximizing principle like utilitarianism, is also known as *maximin*, which stands for "maximizing the minimum." While the difference principle may accept substantial inequalities, the priority it gives to the condition of the worst off is independent of the relative numbers of people in different social positions. It therefore does not permit aggregation of many advantages to the better off to outweigh the disadvantages of a smaller number who are worse off. This will clearly have different policy implications from utilitarianism in a society with a relatively small underclass.

While the pure priority view expresses a sense that it is simply more urgent or more important to improve the condition of those who are in some absolute sense badly off, Rawls's difference principle derives from another moral outlook, identified with a certain idea of fairness. The ruling consideration is that in the design of the social institutions that form the basic structure of society, and that therefore shape everyone's life from birth to death, certain sources of inequality are morally arbitrary—and morally arbitrary inequality cannot be accepted in a just social order, unless it is either unavoidable or justified by some nonarbitrary purpose or end that it serves. So, in Rawls's view, socioeconomic class inequalities are justified only if the system that generates them also does better for the lowest class than any more level system would.

The idea is that a hereditary class structure gives people their start in life and distributes unequal chances from birth, when no one can be said to deserve a better chance than anyone else. The background assumption is that an ideally fair system would give everyone the same chance in life, and that departures from this ideal have to be positively justified. Simply allowing the unequal allocation of possibilities to lie where they fall is not fair, unless it serves some other purpose.

This outlook raises the difficult question, what sources of inequality in the social order, if any, are *non*arbitrary, and therefore do *not* demand rectification?[12] Rawls implies that the familial and social preferences that generate class stratification produce arbitrary inequalities in the life prospects of children born into such a structure. But his most famous and controversial claim is that differences in natural ability—the inequalities of what he calls the natural lottery—have a morally arbitrary effect when they result in differences of earning power. He holds that since no one can be said to deserve the genetic endowment they are born with, desert cannot justify that proportion of difference in material rewards between an unskilled laborer and a highly trained professional that might be attributable to the difference between their genetic endowments. This leaves only people's free choices as a possibly nonarbitrary source of inequality, and Rawls is skeptical that there are feasible institutions that could detect the extent to which people's fortunes are due entirely to their choices. That in turn leads him to support the difference principle, which requires the elimination of all inequalities up to the point where greater equality could only be achieved at the cost of harming the worst off.

Those who do not believe that a general concern for the welfare of all should be one of the ends of government will naturally be opposed to this position, but even many of those who do accept such an end in general terms may find it too egalitarian. Utilitarians, for example, have substantial reasons for favoring a degree of socioeconomic equality, most conspicuously the diminishing marginal utility of resources, which means that if one can transfer a hundred dollars from a rich person to a poor person, the increase in welfare to the latter will greatly exceed the decrease in welfare to the former. However, this argument does not support an absolute priority for improvements to the position of the worst off, independent of the numbers of people in different relevant social positions.

The essential difference is one of theoretical approach. Utilitarians and other maximizers are interested in advancing the total overall welfare, by some appropriate measure. The reduction of inequality is thought of by them as a mere means to the promotion of this end, not as an end in itself. Advocates of a fairness approach, by contrast, are concerned with the terms on which members of a society interact and the social causes that determine their life prospects. They believe that some causes of social and economic inequality are unfair in a sense related to that in which racial or sexual subordination are unfair. This also is behind their view that the effort to reduce those economic inequalities is a requirement of justice, not merely part of the general welfare, and that it therefore deserves the kind of priority in the purposes of government that attaches to the elimination of other injustices, such as racial, religious, or sexual discrimination.

VII. Equality of Opportunity

The appeal to fairness is a deontological as opposed to a consequentialist argument. It can take other forms from the one Rawls gives it. Instead of the difference principle, one might favor the provision of a decent social minimum but cease to worry about giving priority to improvements to the worst off above that level. Or one might concentrate on the provision of equality of opportunity, which would include a certain guarantee of materially decent conditions, health care, and access to education for everyone growing up in the society—while allowing the actual results to depend on the use people made of their opportunities, with differences of ability as well as differences of effort affecting the size of the rewards.

What we believe to be fair and unfair will depend, in a framework of this sort, on what causes of inequality of result we think are morally arbitrary, in a bad sense, and therefore to be eliminated from a just society so far as possible. The most clearly unacceptable sources of inequality in a social order are deliberately imposed caste systems or other

explicit barriers, by which members of certain racial, eth-
nic, religious, or sexual categories are excluded from desirable positions in political, social, or economic life. Next
would come hereditary class stratification, under which
people are born with very unequal life prospects and opportunities simply by virtue of the success or luck of their
parents and grandparents, and the society does nothing to
repair this. Finally, even if a society does a great deal to iron
out such differences of opportunity by providing child support, health care, and good public education for all, there
will remain the large potential inequalities that arise in a
competitive economy as a result of differences in natural
endowment—the ability to acquire scarce productive skills
for which there is high demand in the labor market. Rawls
counts these economic inequalities too as prima facie objectionable, because they are due to genetic characteristics that
people cannot be said to deserve, any more than they deserve
their race, their sex, or their parents' wealth or poverty.

Apart from these very broad questions of social justice,
which obviously bear on the way tax policy should relate to
inequalities of wealth, disposable income, consumption, and
earning power, the aim of avoiding arbitrary sources of inequality can have an influence on the more detailed design of
public policy. In relation to taxes, it manifests itself in controversies over the fairness of differential tax treatment of persons with distinguishing characteristics who are in other ways
economically comparable. The question arises with respect to
savers and spenders, the married and the unmarried, people
with children and people without, and so forth. We shall be
discussing the relation between these smaller-scale questions
of fairness and social justice in chapters 5 and 8.

The examples given so far illustrate the very wide range
of possible views on the legitimate ends of government:
protection of individual rights; pursuit of collective self-
interest by the provision of public goods; promotion of the
general welfare; creation of social and economic justice
through equality of opportunity or redistribution. Evidently,
the implications for tax policy of the position we take on these
issues will be large. The broader the legitimate aims of government, the more it will be entitled to do through design of

the system of property rights to affect the lives of its citizens and the relations among them. The effects will be on a large scale, and individuals will still be free to make personal choices and to determine the course of their lives within the institutional and legal framework created by the state, but depending on the political theory behind the system, that framework may have profound consequences for the range of possibilities that each citizen faces.

VIII.   Legitimate Means and
         Individual Responsibility

Having said something about the ends of government, let us turn in this rough division to the question of legitimate means.

To begin with, it is clear that the aim of distributive justice that we have just been discussing under the heading of ends cannot be separated from a view about the legitimacy of certain means. One cannot maintain that it is an appropriate end of government to maximize the general welfare through the provision of social benefits, or to rectify inequality of opportunity or class stratification, unless one is prepared to countenance the use of taxes to finance those activities, and that means inevitably taxing some people for the benefit of others. How we feel about this will depend on our view of the moral status of private property, as well as on what we think we owe to each other as fellow members of a society.

One view is that taxation is an appropriation by the state of what antecedently belongs to individuals, and that it must overcome a prima facie objection to the transgression of the right of those individuals to dispose of their property as they wish. The opposite view is that what belongs to you is simply defined by the legal system as what you have discretion to dispose of as you wish, after taxes have been levied. Since there are no property rights independent of the tax system, taxes cannot violate those rights. There is no prima facie objection to be overcome, and the tax structure, which forms part of the definition of property rights, along with laws governing contract, gift, inheritance, and so forth, must be evaluated by reference to its effectiveness in promoting legitimate societal goals, including those of distributive justice.

So the dispute over what means are legitimate is in part a dispute over how to describe those means. One party will describe redistributive taxation as forcibly taking what belongs to some and giving it to others; the other party will describe it as using the system of law to institute conventions of property that help realize a just socioeconomic order. But lying behind this dispute is a difference of moral vision, a difference in the role that individual responsibility is thought to play in the justification of a system of property.

As we said in the last chapter, there are very few explicit defenders of radical laissez-faire. But even if one does not adopt the strict libertarian line that property is a completely prepolitical moral concept, and that the state should be designed to protect antecedently valid natural property rights, one may still hold in a Lockean spirit that a significant element of natural or purely moral rights should enter into the design of a system of property, even though the system will also have conventional elements. The main idea of such a position would be that what people own, and what they get in exchange for the work they do under a just social order, should be to a significant degree sensitive to the values of individual responsibility and desert. That would be an argument for the design of a legal system of property rights that reflected the ideal of self-reliance, rather than the ideal of social solidarity.

Someone taking this view would maintain that if people work under a contract for their labor, the moral result in the absence of extraneous considerations is that they deserve to get paid the agreed wage and to keep as much as possible of what they earn. The forcible involvement of a third party, such as the Internal Revenue Service taking a cut, disrupts this morally natural situation and requires special justification. The same would be true if people invest resources that they own in the expectation of a return, but with assumption of risk. The earnings, like the losses, should be theirs, in virtue of the free agreement under which the investment was undertaken. And the same could be said of the exercise of individual discretion in spending or giving away what one owns.

If responsibility and desert should in fact play a major role in determining the design of a just system of property, this will have consequences in two directions. First, it means that the system should encourage rewards for effort and initiative, even beyond what is needed to provide optimal incentives. Second, it should discourage bailing people out of bad situations that are the fault of their own laziness or improvidence, again even beyond what is needed to provide optimal incentives. In other words, some of the tendency toward reducing inequality and helping the worst off will be resisted by a morality of self-reliance and personal desert.

Such an outlook is also naturally allied to the idea that people are entitled to do what they like with what they deserve to have—including giving it to other people they may care about, even if those people have not, similarly, done anything to deserve it. So this view, while it starts from a morality of responsibility and desert, may also support varieties of relatively unimpeded transfer and bequest that generate the type of hereditary class inequality that might otherwise be thought to be undeserved. That poses a threat of moral inconsistency.

However let us put this complication aside for the moment. The central question is whether individual responsibility should be regarded as a fundamental moral factor in the design of a system of taxation, contract, and property rights. Clearly, no workable system could be based entirely on responsibility and desert, since that would require constant interference with property and contract to punish the slothful and reward the industrious. But should it be a factor? That is, should we regard it as a defect of a system that otherwise accomplishes its goals if it takes too much from those who have earned it, or gives too much to those who have not?

IX. Rewards and Punishments

The opposition between two attitudes toward the idea of people deserving or not deserving what they get out of the economy has an analogue in a familiar disagreement about criminal punishment. There, the two attitudes are commonly called retributivism and instrumentalism. The retributivist believes that some people intrinsically deserve to be punished because they have committed certain kinds of wrong against others, and that this is part of the justification of the punishments meted out by the criminal law—a legal enactment of a natural moral demand. Of course, legal punishment also has instrumental value, as a preventive and deterrent. But it is intrinsically justified as well, on this view.

The instrumentalist, by contrast, believes that the entire justification of a system of legal punishments is its efficacy in protecting lives, property, and security. People who commit crimes do deserve to be punished, certainly, but only in the sense that they have no complaint—having acted contrary to rules that serve a useful social purpose and whose violation carries penalties that are needed to maintain those rules. They have no justification for expecting not to be punished if they are caught.

An instrumentalist view about the operation of the economy would be that people deserve the rewards of their labor, or their investments—and also the penalties for their sloth, improvidence, or rashness—but only in the sense that these are legitimate expectations that no one can complain of. If the system under which a labor contract or investment was entered into is just, then the results are legitimate, and a person who ends up with high earnings is fully entitled to them. But this implies no personal moral desert.

The economic analogue of a retributivist doesn't have a convenient name, but it would be someone who believed in natural property rights as a kind of reward for labor and investment and thought it was the job of the state to try to guarantee those rewards, and not just to design the system of property to serve instrumental purposes. Perhaps the most plausible version of this view would assign some intrinsic value to the preservation of a strong link between responsibility and results in the economic system, without claiming that this will determine the larger structure of the system. So there would be a reason other than the need for incentives to want people's rewards to be sensitive to their industry, thrift, postponement of gratification, and so forth.

But is there really a case for moralizing the economic system in this way? The question is whether the justification of rewards essentially in terms of incentives, operating in the context of a system that serves a larger social purpose, is enough, or whether the money people earn should be regarded as theirs in a stronger sense. The need for incentives means that it would be impossible to sever the connection between responsibility and gain or loss. But it would certainly be compatible in principle with radical reduction in the rewards for success and the penalties for failure. That becomes an entirely empirical question about economic effects, not a question of right and wrong.

The same could be said in the opposite direction about rewards that are sometimes criticized as too large, like the compensation of star athletes, entertainers, and CEO's. Those who think responsibility and desert should play no independent role in evaluating the system will reply that such astronomical salaries can be judged only by comparing the total system that generates them with some comprehensive alternative: comparing them instrumentally, in the results they produce for society as a whole. Rewards taken in isolation cannot be identified as deserved or undeserved.

On balance, it doesn't seem either necessary or possible to make sense of the overall profile of economic compensation in a modern society in terms of moral desert, as if it were a more positive analogue of the criminal justice system. There is still room for the pure value of responsibility for the consequences of one's choices, even in a system that determines the possibilities and alternatives on more comprehensive instrumental grounds. Relative to the background situation, we can say that two people who make different choices to work, save, invest, etc. are responsible for the results, insofar as the situation gives them grounds to form expectations on which their choices can be based. It is a good thing if people have in this sense some control over their lives, and if the economic system provides them with alternatives in virtue of which they can be responsible for the consequences of their choices.[13] That is inseparable from the value of individual freedom and self-determination, which persists even in highly structured environments.

But none of this means that the value of individual responsibility can itself determine the basic socioeconomic structure. Individual freedom and responsibility are preserved so long as there is *some* system of private property and choice of employment. Taxes and transfer payments do not automatically erode individual responsibility: They merely change the conditions under which it has to be exercised. The money you earn under any system is yours because you have worked for it, but it is a mistake to think that what you have really earned is your pretax income, some of which the government then comes and takes away from you.

It may be that the real objection to redistribution, from those who appeal to responsibility, is that it is not legitimate for the state to hold us all collectively responsible for one another—for one another's welfare or for everyone's getting a fair start in life. That is a disagreement about ends, rather than about means. On this view, the setting up of the framework in which we interact and make our choices should not undermine each person's sole responsibility for himself, by imposing a collective responsibility for others through the implementation of an egalitarian conception of justice. And insofar as the addition of responsibility for others diminishes the scope of each person's responsibility for himself, this could be regarded as an objection from the erosion of individual responsibility. To give priority to the maximization of individual responsibility in this sense, over other values with which it may conflict, such as the promotion of the general welfare and equality of opportunity, essentially amounts to denying that we have responsibility for one another through the agency of the state.

X. Liberty and Libertarianism

There is another type of value related to the subject of responsibility, however, namely, the value of liberty and autonomy of the individual—freedom from interference or undue pressure in pursuing one's own course in life. This is recognized as a good by consequentialist as well as deontological theories. Indeed, John Stuart Mill argued in *On Liberty* that if our ultimate standard of social value is promotion of the general happiness, the preservation of individual liberty is a vital means to that end, since it allows people to discover experimentally on their own what will make them happy, and thus leads to development over time of improved forms and conditions of life. This implies that any government incursion into economic life should leave people free to express their preferences as flexibly as possible through their economic choices, and should avoid constraining the options, unless that is unavoidable.

But liberty can also play a quite different role in deontological theories, not as a goal but as a limitation on what may be done in the pursuit of other goals. One of the most important strains in modern political theory is the idea that the authority of the state over the individual is not unlimited, however worthy may be the goal for which the state's power is exercised. Individuals, on this view, retain a certain degree of sovereignty over themselves, even when they are members of a collective social order. They may be constrained by majority decision in some respects and for some purposes but not in others.

The most familiar protections of this kind are the basic personal rights: freedom of expression, freedom of religion, freedom of association, privacy, and the protection of the person against physical violation. These are standard elements of any liberal position. But there are also those who would include some form of economic freedom in the protected category, and that has significant implications for the subject of taxation.

Clearly, a minimal form of economic freedom is essential to a liberal system: the freedom to hold personal property with discretion to do what one wants with it. The question, though, is whether a much larger economic freedom than this—freedom to engage with minimal hindrance or conditions in significant economic activity of the sort that drives a market economy—belongs with the basic human rights as part of the authority that each of us ought to retain over our own lives. If so, government incursion on that liberty through fiscal policy would be suspect and might require exceptionally strong justification.

In the extreme libertarian version of this view, the only justification for such interference would be the protection of these and other comparably important individual rights themselves. Thus, government interference with economic liberty through taxation would be justified to support national defense, a judiciary, and a police force, in order to ensure that freedom and security are preserved and contract and property rights enforced. No taxation merely to promote the general welfare, or to secure distributive justice or equality of opportunity, would be permissible.

But even if one does not take the libertarian sanctification of economic liberty that far, it would be possible to hold a position with libertarian elements, according to which restrictions of economic freedom were prima facie objectionable, so that taxation for the general good could be justified only in exceptional cases. It seems clear that some of the political opposition to taxes in the United States reflects such an outlook. And as we argued in chapter 2, an unexamined "everyday" libertarianism seems to be a tacit assumption of much of the traditional tax policy literature.

The view is that government should make it easy for individuals to engage in cooperative economic activity, by protecting property and seeing that contracts are enforced, but that it should not constrain the forms of those activities or encumber them with collateral conditions like taxes or zoning or environmental regulations unless absolutely necessary—because people should have a right to do what they wish with their property provided they don't hurt others. Sometimes these laissez-faire policies are also supported on consequentialist grounds—as best for the general welfare—but they usually reflect a rights-based, deontological political morality.

The division of opinion here is fundamental. Egalitarian liberals simply see no moral similarity between the right to speak one's mind, to practice one's religion, or to act on one's sexual inclinations, and the right to enter into a labor contract or a sale of property unencumbered by a tax bite. Denying the latter, they believe, is just not the kind of interference with autonomy that centrally threatens people's control over their lives. Some forms of personal discretion—including the basic

Hegelian right to hold personal property—are at the core of the self, but unimpeded economic freedom is not one of them.

Libertarians, however, are convinced that the government's sticking its hands into a transaction between private individuals, raising its cost by requiring that some percentage of what is exchanged be diverted to the public treasury, is a gross incursion on personal liberty, justifiable only for grave reasons, like those that justify the use of police power to prevent crime.

The libertarian conception of property as a prepolitical moral notion is based not on the idea of moral desert but rather on the idea of moral entitlement. Each person, on this view, is in certain respects inviolable. It may not make sense to say that we deserve to be who we are and to have the capacities and endowments we have, but they are ours, to use as we see fit. Our original sovereignty over ourselves—a moral given, not created by the state—leaves us free to employ our capacities and implies that others have no right to interfere with that freedom, unless in using it we transgress the rights of others.

The state cannot change this. It is not a collective arrangement whereby we all own shares in each other, which we can exploit for the common good. Rather, each of us has the right to decide what to do with our own capacities, and how to dispose of the product of any enterprise, individual or cooperative, that we have voluntarily undertaken. The state has no more right to demand a cut of the profits for redistribution in exchange for its maintenance of the peaceful conditions of cooperation than it would have to demand adherence to a particular religion for the same reason. To champion other liberal rights while belittling economic freedom is morally inconsistent. That is the libertarian position. Though we are out of sympathy with it, it evidently has considerable appeal and exercises a real influence in political debate.

XI. The Moral Significance of the Market

These deep disagreements express themselves in conflicts over the moral significance of the market—one of the most important institutions of our common world. Much of what can be said about it concerns its instrumental value in combining the information from countless individual choices to make possible the efficient use of resources in the invention, production, and distribution of things people need and want. There is also much to be said about conditions in which the market fails, often as a result of externalities that require more centralized intervention to prevent the production of an evil like pollution or to promote a good like public transport.

But in addition to producing and distributing goods and services, the market economy also distributes income and wealth, through the labor market and through the return on investment. It is this feature that poses moral questions, some of which we have discussed already. In the course of its other functions, the market generates economic inequalities, partly through differences between people's productive contributions, partly through the differential performance of investments, partly through parental largesse—and all these inequalities raise questions about whether their causes are sufficient to make them morally legitimate. Those who think not will be inclined to favor some degree of taxation for redistributive purposes, as well as for the provision of public goods.

There is another aspect to the moral significance of the market, that remains even after broad questions of socioeconomic inequality have been dealt with. Those distributive questions arise when we look at the effects of a market economy on a large scale. But there is also the small scale, that is, the way that people's choices in a market economy affect their individual lives and make them personally responsible, up to a point, for the course their life takes among the options available.

Of course, the options provided by the system are limited, and important questions of justice arise about what should be done to modify them. But if broad conditions of distributive justice and equality of opportunity are met, then it may be that a market economy has merit not only on grounds of efficiency, but also because it gives people responsibility for the shape of their own lives and makes their consumption of various goods, their leisure, their savings, how hard they work, what material luxuries they enjoy depend on their choices among alternative mixtures of such things.

Equally significant, it makes the consequences of each person's choices also sensitive to the interests of others, in a desirable way. If I use my resources to acquire a scarce good that many others also want, I will have to pay more for it than if I want something for which there is little demand and which is easily available. If I want more of what others want, I will have to sacrifice leisure, doing work that others want done, to acquire the resources to get it.

In sum, the market can be given a moral interpretation as a mechanism that makes each of us as economic actors responsible for the allocation of effort and resources in our own lives, and that makes the benefits we derive from those choices systematically dependent on their costs and benefits to others.[14] It can even be seen as putting people in a position of equality with respect to one another, so that the differences that emerge between them will all be the result of their exercise of an equal freedom from an initial starting point of equality.[15]

The trouble with this ideal picture is that in the real world, people do not enter the market equipped with equal resources or equal skills or equal talents. They have some responsibility for what they make of their situation through their employment, investment, and expenditure decisions, but it is responsibility against the background of unequal starting points or circumstances of choice. Still, even if the problems of equality of opportunity and distributive justice require separate treatment, a market economy as a structure of interaction can be thought of as having its own value, provided it is not the only mechanism determining the allocation of economic benefits. That means that there is no incompatibility between this justification of the market, as a way of realizing the value of individual responsibility, and the inclusion in the system of taxes that modify the background conditions of choice. Taxes that are used to fund programs that promote distributive justice or equality of opportunity help to purify the relation between the market and personal responsibility, rather than undermining it.

But the most important function of a market economy in any conception of justice is not as an end in itself, but as a means to the encouragement of production and the generation of wealth. The price system is the site of the incentives that motivate people to do what is needed to sustain a productive modern economy, and the mechanism by which resources and labor are allocated to different purposes. Therefore, the potential distortionary effect of taxes on prices and economic incentives is a large part of any debate over the rights and wrongs of tax policy.

Much of the public debate is over the empirical question of what effects different taxes will have on productivity, employment, and the health of the economy—including distortionary consequences and losses of efficiency. The issues here are familiar: alleged trickle-down effects of reduced progressivity—advantages to ordinary wage-earners of the stimulus to innovation and investment if high earnings are less heavily taxed; the effects on the mobility of capital of taxing capital gains at a lower rate than other earnings; the effects of the separate corporate income tax, and the value of accelerated depreciation allowances as a tax incentive to investment.

Perennially interesting is the question of the effect of the marginal rate of income tax on earners at various levels. In theory, there should be two conflicting behavioral influences: the substitution effect, whereby people work less hard (substituting leisure for work) if their expected after-tax return per hour is lower; and the income effect, that is, the lowering of their disposable income, which in turn gives them a motive to work harder.[16] Since an increase in the marginal rate of tax will both reduce some people's disposable income and reduce their after-tax return for an extra hour of work, it will have both these effects, and it is not clear which will dominate, at any given level of income and taxation. Presumably, the substitution effect will be dominant for people who have a lot of money, and the opposite effect will be dominant for people who have very little, but in between it is not so clear. Still, this suggests that marginal tax rates that decline with income may have something to be said for them, so that inequalities might be more effectively dealt with by direct transfer payments rather than by steeply progressive taxation. We will take up all these issues in subsequent chapters.

XII. Personal Motives and Political Values: The Moral Division of Labor

But there is another aspect to the problem of incentives that is especially interesting for normative political theory: the disparity it reveals between personal and political motivation and values.[17]

Any political system that uses taxation as an instrument for the realization of a conception of social justice has harnessed the promotion of the collective social good to the economic activity that results when individual members of the society pursue their separate economic interests, thus creating wealth. The income or profits that are taxed are the results of essentially self-interested private activity; they are not generated by their earners in order to provide resources for the public treasury. And the design of tax policy simply assumes that, whatever taxes people face, they will consider primarily their own private interests and not those of the society as a whole in making their economic decisions.

That is why incentive arguments can take the form, for example, of defending less progressive income tax rates with the claim that this will induce the highly skilled and inventive to engage in more productive and entrepreneurial activity. It is not thought reasonable, even by egalitarian liberals, to expect people to work equally hard whatever the rate of taxation, just in order to generate lots of money for the internal revenue.

So the typical liberal system, which combines a market economy with various redistributive policies, is based on a stark division between personal and political motives. As supporters of the system, it asks people to accept policies whose aim is the general welfare, justice, fairness, or some more precise conception of social value. As individuals, on the other hand, it assumes they will look out for themselves and the other people they particularly care about, rather than considering the interests of all, fairly balanced against one another.

There is, in other words, a division of labor between individuals and social institutions with respect to the promotion of social justice. There is disagreement among philosophers over whether this reflects a fundamental division between the moral principles governing individual conduct and the principles governing the design of social institutions. Some think those institutions are inherently required to display an impartiality among the interests of individuals, or a concern to combat certain kinds of inequality, that is quite different from the concerns that individuals are required to have for their fellows, when they are not acting in the role of citizens.

On this "discontinuity" view, roughly, individuals as individuals can be strongly partial toward themselves and their families vis-à-vis strangers, provided they don't directly harm others or otherwise violate their rights; but the state must pursue the interests of all its citizens according to some standard of fairness or equality and may obligate individuals to contribute to this impartial end through taxation and various redistributive policies. Moreover as citizens, individuals are morally obliged to support such impartial public institutions, even though they can remain strongly partial in private life. In other words, there are two moralities, one for individuals and one for society.

The contrasting, "continuity" view is that the same fundamental moral standards underlie the requirements on individuals and institutions, but that the division of labor between social institutions and individual responsibility is the most effective way to promote the ends of morality—those ends being a decent condition of life for everyone, the elimination of serious social inequalities, and an opportunity for each person to flourish by pursuing individual aims and interests within the framework of a just system. In other words, there is a single morality, but it justifies a complex division of responsibilities between individuals and society.[18]

Both of these views attempt to dissolve what may at first seem like a paradox in the functioning of modern liberal democratic institutions: the radical division between the sorts of motives they call on in asking for political support, particularly from the more fortunate, and the motives they suppose will govern individuals in their private and professional lives. Does it really make sense—is it psychologically coherent—for people to be acquisitive, competitive, and dedicated to advancing the interests of themselves and their families in their personal lives while being impartially concerned with the interests of all, and with reducing inequalities between families, in their political choices—choices, for example, to support taxes on themselves for the benefit of others?[19]

Even if it is not incoherent, the contrast between private partiality and public impartiality creates problems when it comes to maintaining political support for programs to secure socioeconomic justice. Such programs will not survive politically, in a typical modern democracy, unless they are supported not only by their economic beneficiaries but also by at least some of those whose taxes will have to pay for them and who would be left with more after-tax income under a less generous regime. In individual conduct, it is assumed that these people, like everyone else, will try every legal means to minimize their taxes. Why then will they sometimes support laws that increase those taxes? It is partly because they want the laws to tax other people; but it isn't only that. Many people seem to be comfortable with a moral division of labor that mostly deputizes the tax and transfer system to express their commitment to social justice, leaving them free in private life to be as self-indulgent as they may wish to be.

The political problem of taxes is that it is risky for a politician to attempt to appeal to these better angels of our nature—the ones motivated by fairness and impartiality. When it comes to taxes, at least in the United States, there seems to be a premium on appeals to the selfishness and greed of the voter. It is not clear how a transformation in the public conscience might be achieved, which would make socioeconomic justice less dangerous as an argument for taxation. In the present climate, the alternative is to avoid programs that specifically benefit the worst off and to offer broader forms of social assistance that can be thought of as benefiting a majority.

On the other hand, this may reflect a widespread moral conviction that we do not owe each other more help or more impartial concern through the state than we do as individuals, and that each of us is entitled to form our political preferences on the same basically self-interested grounds that govern our private economic choices. At any rate, the issues should be clear.

XIII. Conclusion

The values that bear on the assessment of public policy are very diverse, so there is much to disagree about. First, there are questions about the legitimate ends of public policy— whether they should be defined by collective self-interest, or the general welfare, or some conception of fairness, including equal opportunity. Each of these in turn needs to be further defined, particularly with respect to the correct way to combine or balance out the distinct interests of many different people. Second, there are questions about the limits on the authority of the state over the individual, and whether property rights have any part in defining those limits, or whether they are mere conventions designed for other purposes. Third, there are questions about the proper role of responsibility and desert in the determination of people's economic rewards—and about what individuals can and cannot be held responsible for. Fourth, there are questions about the importance of equality of opportunity, and its relation to inherited economic inequality—and the broader question of what social causes of distributive inequality should be regarded as offensively arbitrary. Finally, there are questions about the importance of freedom of choice in economic life.

Issues of taxation, in particular, will turn on the economic interpretation of both individual autonomy and interpersonal responsibility—the two major poles of the problem of political legitimacy and justice. What kind of concern do we owe our fellow citizens, and what in our lives should remain free of collective control? It is these sorts of values, in conjunction with factual assumptions, that must be appealed to in justifying a tax structure, and the overall system of property rights of which it is an inextricable part.

The conviction that determines our approach to all more specific questions is that there are no property rights antecedent to the tax structure. Property rights are the product of a set of laws and conventions, of which the tax system forms a part. Pretax income, in particular, has no independent moral significance. It does not define something to which the taxpayer has a prepolitical or natural right, and which the government expropriates from the individual in levying taxes on it. All the normative questions about what taxes are justified and what taxes are unjustified should be interpreted instead as questions about how the system should define those property rights that arise through the various transactions—employment, bequest, contract, investment, buying and selling—that are subject to taxation.

Putting it this way will bring up many of the same considerations that arise in more traditional versions of the debate, but they will be applied to the evaluation of the entire system of rules and its results, not to the justification of incursion on a presumed natural right. People do have a right to their income, but its moral force depends on the background of procedures and institutions against which they have acquired that income—procedures that are fair only if they include taxation to support various forms of equality of opportunity, public goods, distributive justice, and so forth. Since income gives rise to clear moral entitlement only if the system under which it is earned, including taxes, is fair, entitlement to income cannot be used as an assumption to evaluate the fairness of the tax system.

While this conventionalism seems to us just like common sense, we recognize that it goes against a natural illusion of a kind that arises whenever the conventions governing a practice are so pervasive and deeply buried that they become invisible. It is true of the conventions of language, which seem natural, even though we know they are highly arbitrary. To say that the pig is rightly so called—on account of its eating habits and tendency to wallow in the mud—would be a joke: treating the conventional meaning of the word as a fact of nature, and then using it to justify the convention, in other words to justify itself.

The conventionality of property is even more elusive than the conventionality of language, and it is easy to lose hold of the idea that the wage for which you agree to sell your labor, and which your employer agrees to pay you, is merely a bookkeeping figure. It has only an indirect relation to the property rights over disposable income that will result from that transaction under the existing legal system, and what it legally entitles you to is morally legitimate only by virtue of the legitimacy of the system. Conventionalism keeps being pushed aside under pressure from an unanalyzed simple intuition of what is mine and what is yours. But that intuition in fact depends on the background of a system of property law: it can't be used to evaluate the system.

Evaluation must decide how "mine" and "yours" ought to be determined; it cannot start with a set of assumptions about what is mine and what is yours. The right answer will depend on what system best serves the legitimate aims of society with legitimate means and without imposing illegitimate costs. That is the only way an essentially conventional system of property, and therefore a tax scheme, can be justified. The justification may refer to considerations of individual liberty, desert, and responsibility as well as to general welfare, equality of opportunity, and so forth. But it cannot appeal, at the fundamental level, to property rights.

4

Redistribution and Public Provision

We begin our discussion of the more substantive issues of tax policy by considering a major division between two kinds of contribution made to the character of a society by any regime of taxation—consequences which together raise many of the philosophical issues of social justice that we have identified.

Taxation has two primary functions. (1) It determines how much of a society's resources will come under the control of government, for expenditure in accordance with some collective decision procedure, and how much will be left in the discretionary control of private individuals, as their personal property. Call this *public-private division*. (2) It plays a central role in determining how the social product is shared out among different individuals, both in the form of private property and in the form of publicly provided benefits. Call this *distribution*.

Even though many tax-supported programs perform both of these functions, they are conceptually distinct. It is important to keep the distinction in mind in thinking about taxes, because it is not just conceptual but normative. Reasons for and against putting resources under government rather than private control are not necessarily reasons for or against redistributing resources among groups or individuals, and vice versa. Political rhetoric tends to identify big government with egalitarian redistribution, but there is no necessary connection between positions on the two issues.

One might favor a strongly egalitarian distributive policy of money transfers or cash subsidies while being against all but a minimal level of public provision—leaving individuals as free as possible to determine how their share of the social product is to be expended. On the other hand, one might be in favor of a high level of public provision, including public education, health care, military expenditure, environmental and social control, support for science, art, sport, entertainment, and culture, while not being in favor of any redistribution, except that which occurs as an inevitable side-effect of the financing of these goods by the unequal taxation of persons with unequal resources. Of course, one might also be hostile to both redistribution and public provision or favorable to both; the point is only that the correlation is not necessary, and we won't get a clear view of the reasons bearing on the two questions if we don't distinguish them.

But there is another reason for distinguishing distribution from public-private division, and it is this: We cannot evaluate different answers to the public-private question, except by reference to some answer to the distribution question that is taken as already given, because we cannot compare the value of public and private use of resources unless we know how the private control of those resources will be distributed among individuals if they are not used publicly.

Efficiency requires that we not employ resources publicly if their private use would do more good, and vice versa: Ideally, the boundary between the two should be drawn in a way that equalizes the marginal value, by some appropriate measure, of public and private expenditures. But if the private distribution that provides the alternative to public expenditure is unjust, that will distort the comparison: The value of public expenditure will be compared with the value of the "wrong" private expenditures. What we want, ideally, is to be able to compare public with private expenditure under a regime of distribution that can be assumed to be just among individuals.

Some public expenditures are themselves redistributive in effect, but even with respect to those that are not, we can only address the public-private question in light of some answer to the problem of distribution. That problem, as we saw in the last chapter, is the subject of massive disagreement. There are many conceptions of distributive justice, in varying degrees egalitarian, utilitarian, and/or liberal. Moreover, their implementation will always involve some public expenditure, at least for maintenance of the legal system and provision of external and domestic security, but often much more than that. Yet we need to assume at least some notional solution to the distribution problem before we can evaluate the possible levels and methods of financing of public expenditures such as these.

This will be a purely imaginary allocation of resources among individuals, representing a particular conception of justice. Any real allocation, by contrast, will be the result of some combination of private economic interaction under appropriate conditions of liberty and opportunity, perhaps some degree of taxation and transfer, some forms of direct public provision, and differential taxation. But the desired form of these mechanisms cannot be determined independently of distributive assumptions, because we cannot evaluate a public expenditure except by comparing it with the value of the private use to which those resources would otherwise be put—and to do that we have to know who would get those resources.

It isn't clear how best to think about this mutual interdependence of the two elements of taxation. Any distributive aim will depend for its implementation on some form of public-private division, and any public-private division can be justified only against the background of some distributive assumption. This is not going to be a simple matter of solving a pair of simultaneous equations. The interrelationships are too complicated.

First, if we could assume a just distribution as a starting point, then we would want to set the level and type of non-distributive public provision—essentially public goods—so that people will get their money's worth, allocating to the public sector only as much as could not be better used if left, justly distributed, in private hands. Second, whatever our conception of distributive justice, we cannot implement a just system of distribution without some public expenditures, so those expenditures cannot be evaluated in the same way against the background of the just distribution that requires them as a condition. Third, some and perhaps most forms of public provision will combine the distributive and non-distributive functions, especially through the way they are financed by differential taxation, so they will both create the background conditions for their evaluation and be evaluated by reference to them. Fourth, whatever taxes are levied to pay for public provision on the assumption of a just distribution will have secondary effects (distortionary effects, so-called) on production and distribution, perhaps rendering the assumption false and requiring compensatory adjustments. All this creates an almost impenetrable tangle of justification.

And yet it seems a desirable aim to treat distribution and public-private division to some extent separately—to want to arrange things so that individuals get their just share of the social product and so that the marginal dollar of public expenditure, in the benefits it produces, is worth the sacrifice in private expenditure that would otherwise be possible, under a fair allocation. Classical theorists like Knut Wicksell and Erik Lindahl dealt with the problem by simply assuming a just distribution among individuals, without specifying how it was produced, and evaluating tax and public expenditure policies as if they were departures from that benchmark.[1]

II. Paying for Public Goods

Any allocation of the entire social product among individuals is a fiction, whether it is assumed to be just or not. Some public expenditure is needed to sustain a legal and economic order of any kind. But let us as a thought experiment suppose a notional division of control over resources among individuals in a society, and let us for the moment bracket the question of distribution by simply assuming this division is just, by some standard.

The standard might even be the minimal one associated with libertarianism, according to which the distribution of the social product is just, provided it is arrived at under conditions of natural liberty—through uncoerced economic transactions and free gifts and exchanges under a system of law that permits everyone to participate and enforces their property rights equally. For present purposes, we are thinking of it not in its strict libertarian form, which would prohibit compulsory taxation, but rather as a distributive baseline for the financing of public goods. Essentially, this would mean that there are no substantive standards of distributive justice, only procedural ones, and that justice per se doesn't require any redistribution at all, even to ensure equality of opportunity.[2]

But we could also suppose that the just distribution requires a social minimum, or equality of opportunity, or some stronger principle of equality. We will assume only that, however egalitarian in spirit the conception is, a just distribution will still involve substantial inequality of resources. This is simple realism. But we will leave indeterminate for now the nature of a just distribution, in order to focus on public provision. Since any substantive conception of distributive justice will in practice have to be realized partly through public provision, the two topics will have to be rejoined later.

If some solution to the distribution problem is assumed to be in the background, the main reason for public provision will be to supply public goods—that is, those from the benefit of which individuals cannot be excluded, because they cannot be supplied for anyone unless they are supplied for everyone. These will include such things as external and domestic security and the maintenance of the legal system which permits natural liberty to govern the creation and distribution of resources, but also perhaps various other cultural, social, and environmental goods that make a difference to the quality of life.

There is one complication that we shall note here but then set aside: Not everyone will "consume" each of these public goods to the same extent. The Coast Guard and hurricane warnings, for example, have limited value for residents of Nebraska—though tornado alerts may help to even things out. Political horse-trading can sometimes deal with this problem in a rough-and-ready way, since there are many different public goods competing for resources. The division of the tax base for different purposes among local, state, and national populations may also help to ensure that people are getting the public goods they pay for. However, we will disregard this complication in the discussion that follows and count as a public good any good that cannot be supplied to specific individuals but must be made generally available if it is to be provided at all.

We will also set aside for the moment a different reason for public expenditure that might appropriately be called *public duties*. Though not everyone would agree, the view is fairly widespread that—quite apart from any requirement of distributive justice—we have some form of collective obligation to contribute to the prevention or alleviation of major disasters like famines, epidemics, and environmental degradation, and perhaps that we also have an obligation to support certain intrinsic goods like art (including preservation of the artistic heritage). Such obligations, if they exist, transcend national boundaries, and they may be strict enough to be forcibly imposed by governments on their citizens. That would be a justification for taxing people to provide foreign aid to severely impoverished countries or government support for the arts, based not on the benefit these things provide for the citizenry but on a duty citizens have to support them.

We shall return to this topic later, but for now we shall concentrate on public goods that are goods *for* the public. And we have bracketed the distributive question by assuming for the sake of argument an unequal but just distribution as the background.

In determining the level and type and form of financing of each of these public goods, we will also be determining what is left under the private control of each individual. And if the prior distribution is just, we should want appropriations out of it for these public purposes to give people their money's worth. Since exclusion isn't possible, we can't do this by asking everyone to purchase only the amount of military protection, for example, that they want and feel they can afford. Nor can we offer protection at the same price for everyone, excluding those who don't pay. We have to give everyone the same level of protection, at the same per capita cost in public expenditure, even though its monetary value to each of them will be different.

The main reason for this difference in value is not that some people care more about the dangers of military invasion than others, but that some people have more money than others, so that a dollar more taken from them to be spent on defense does not mean a dollar less for basic necessities, but only for something less important. The more money you have, the less a marginal dollar is worth to you, so the marginal utility of your expenditures on defense and on alternative private purposes will be equalized at a higher level than they will for someone who has considerably less—under the unequal but presumptively just distribution that is our benchmark.

The best we can do, therefore, is to set public expenditure at a level financed by unequal contributions from individuals that come as close as possible to equalizing the marginal utility of public and private expenditure for each of them. At any given level of total defense spending, the resulting protection will be worth more money to those who have plenty of it than to those who don't, so this means efficiency will be promoted if the former pay more. Of course, these values simply have to be guessed at by the designers of the system, since they won't be revealed by a market. Whether they could be revealed by the political process is a difficult question.

This is completely different from the pricing and allocation of goods in the free market. If a good like asparagus can be bought by one individual without being supplied to everyone, and if there is a competitive market for its supply, then two things will follow. First, people who differ in wealth or income but who are equally partial to asparagus will buy more or less or none of it at a given price. Second, all buyers will be able to get it at the same price—which for some is the maximum they would be willing to pay for a few spears of asparagus, but for others, wealthier than they, is well below the maximum or reserve price they would be willing to pay, even for all the asparagus they could possibly eat. A competitive market in private goods therefore automatically creates a large surplus—the difference between actual price and reserve price—for people who have lots of money. Poor people benefit from this surplus only with very cheap private goods like salt and digital watches. To them, most things don't feel cheap or costless, because most purchases are close to their reserve price.

With a public good, individuals can't obtain different amounts of it and there is no need to charge everyone the same, so there is no automatic radically unequal allocation of surplus. The question for the state then becomes what *single* amount of the good to provide to everybody, and at what *separate* price for each? This is very different from the question facing the producer of a private good: what *single* price to charge everyone so that total sales, of *unequal* amounts to different individuals, will yield maximum profit? The government must operate more like a price-discriminating monopoly. It needs to figure out how much the public good is worth to each individual and charge each of them accordingly, financing the total cost of the good out of the sum of the unequal assessments and setting the level of provision at a point where for each person the assessment is less than or equal to that person's reserve price for that level.

Some high levels of public provision will fail to meet this condition, because they cost more than the sum of what they are worth to all the individuals whose taxes must pay for them. There will be no way of distributing their costs so that their marginal utility will not be lower than that of alternative private uses of that money by at least some taxpayers. On the other hand, some low levels of public provision will be clearly inefficient, because they necessarily leave at least some taxpayers in the private possession of money that would give them greater marginal utility if it were taxed away from them to provide a higher level of provision.

In between will fall levels of provision and allocation of costs that are efficient and that do not exceed any taxpayer's reserve price. For these solutions, one will not be able to improve anyone's situation by a change in their taxes or in the level of public provision without worsening someone else's situation. However, since many solutions are efficient in this sense, efficiency alone will not dictate a choice among them. Even if taxpayers contribute unequally to the cost of public goods, in accordance with the different value to them of money, there will in most cases still be a surplus that can be distributed among them in different ways. That is because the total cost of a public good will usually be lower than the sum of the reserve prices of individuals for a given level of provision. So there will be levels of national security, say, or street cleaning, whose cost can be covered by more than one division among taxpayers without exceeding anyone's reserve price. Indeed, there may be many kinds of public goods of which this is true at any level of provision up to the satiation level—that is, the level at which the marginal utility drops to zero and no one would want any more battleships or street cleaners at any price.

Suppose there is a satiation level for national defense, and that Poor were willing to pay at a maximum 10% of a $20,000 income to reach that level, and Rich were willing to pay up to 30% of a $100,000 income, but that the cost per citizen of this level is only $10,000. Clearly, it would be inefficient to take $10,000 out of the private consumption of each of them to finance it, since that would make Poor worse off. It would also be inefficient to choose a lower level of provision. But if this level is supplied by the state, should Poor be assessed $2,000 and Rich $18,000; or should Rich pay $20,000 and Poor nothing; or should each pay a share of the total in proportion to their reserve prices—that is, $18,750 and $1,250? (Not that those are the only efficient alternatives.) All these allocations not only are efficient but also equalize the marginal utility of defense and private expenditure for each taxpayer—since the marginal utility of a defense dollar for each depends on how much the other is paying.

This choice by the state in its role as a nonprofit price-discriminating monopoly does, inevitably, bring up questions of fairness and not just efficiency. It may be a kind of fairness that is not identical with distributive justice, since it can clearly arise even against the background of a distribution that is not subjected to standards of the latter sort. But even a libertarian will not be able to leave to the market, or an imaginary market, the pricing of public goods.[3] So we see that distributive questions are unavoidably involved in the problem of public provision, even for those who don't in the ordinary sense believe in distributive justice.

Assessment in proportion to benefit, as measured by different reserve prices, does seem a plausible standard, and this would probably be in effect significantly progressive. So there is room for something like the benefit principle, which we earlier rejected as a general principle of tax justice, in this restricted context. Against the background of a distribution which is assumed to be just, the funding of public goods may best be arranged according to some standard of proportionality to benefit. However, this is only one possibility: other theories of distributive justice may bear on the choice more directly.

But even though a distributive element enters these choices because of the surplus, it is important to recognize that substantial inequalities in the allocation of tax support for public goods will be dictated by efficiency alone, given a background of unequal distribution of resources. The efficient allocations of cost among which we must choose are already significantly unequal, in ways that correspond to the background inequality. (In the above example, they fall between 18,000/2,000 and 20,000/0.)

There is a sense in which such a system will inevitably seem redistributive in effect, if not in intent. To take another example, if the rich would be happy to pay a lot for clean streets and the poor very little, the poor will get them anyway, largely paid for by taxes on the rich, at a level that the poor could not afford on their own. But the alternative is either that the poor be required to pay more for street-cleaning than it is worth to them, or that the rich get dirty streets in exchange for extra disposable income that is worth less to them than it would be if spent on clean streets. So what is driving the solution is really efficiency, not redistribution.

III. Which Goods Are Public?

Partisans of the market are inclined to see greater efficiency in the minimization of public expenditure and the provision of as many goods as possible through private contract. Thomas Schelling has even suggested that poor people should be allowed to patronize cheaper airlines and airports that offer a lower level of safety than rich people require—since it would be worth the savings to them.[4] In money terms, after all, rich people value their lives much more than poor people do. Often, however, there is no satisfactory individualized substitute for public goods—not only those of the minimal nightwatchman state but others as well. Rich people can band together in restricted private communities, where the streets are clean and the landscaping and security perfect, but this isn't enough, even for them. They also want to be able to live and work in safe and attractive cities with diverse populations. Leaving everything to the market will in certain respects leave everyone worse off than they could otherwise be.

It may be that the justification of public provision not for purposes of redistribution but rather to provide public goods for reasons of efficiency—goods that benefit everyone—can be extended to cover a great deal. The classic public goods are defense, domestic security, the legal system, environmental protection, and public health. But there may be important aesthetic, social, and cultural goods that cannot be supplied privately. If we can ensure a decent level of education for all, independently of their ability to pay, the result will be a society that is much better for everyone to live in, and economically better for almost everyone, than a society with high levels of illiteracy and innumeracy. Whether it is achieved through public schools or through mandated education underwritten by subsidies or vouchers, the benefits are not limited to the direct recipients. A considerable support for universal education by the haves, even with minimal tax contribution from the have-nots, will produce on balance a result that is advantageous for the haves as well as the have-nots, in both social and economic terms.

Similar things could be said of support for the performing arts in order to foster a creative cultural environment, support for scientific and scholarly research, and so forth. Finally, there is also a case, based on this type of efficiency consideration, for traditional social welfare policies guaranteeing a decent minimum standard of living, or decent minimum earnings, for everyone in the society. Such programs are usually regarded as redistributive, but the alternative to a decent social minimum is a society with real poverty, which often results in higher rates of crime, drug addiction, and single motherhood, all of which impose their own costs not only on the poor but on everyone. To be grim about it, the cost of subsidizing wages for unskilled labor to make them sufficient to support a family might well be balanced by savings in the costs of prisons and law enforcement that such a change would produce, not to mention the value for everyone of the change in the social environment.[5]

Again, such programs would not be redistributive in the usual sense of benefiting some at the expense of others. The poor would benefit but only to the extent that the rich would also. The size of the benefit to the poor would depend on what would equalize marginal benefit to the rich from among competing categories of expenditure—how much the well-to-do could contribute before alternative uses of their money, including private consumption, would be more valuable to them—the diametrical opposite of Rawls's difference principle.

The reduction of social and economic inequality is in this way seen as a public good, paid for according to its monetary value to different individual taxpayers. This case differs from that of national defense, for example, in that it makes no sense to tax the poor for some of the cost of raising their spendable income. But it is still driven by efficiency, not fairness—a direct appeal to the interests of each, with no sacrifice being imposed on anyone. There are obvious political advantages in portraying social welfare policies in this way, but that doesn't mean there is nothing in it.

If, however, the efficiency arguments go in the other direction and favor the construction of prisons over provision of a social minimum—or if, for whatever reason, the well off are not unhappy to live in a society full of poor people (it solves the servant problem), then we have to consider the question of distribution independently. So far in this chapter we have been asking how to determine the appropriate level of public provision relative to minimal assumptions about the standards of justice that a distribution of resources among private individuals must meet. That includes the libertarian standard. Now we have to consider more restrictive alternatives to that background assumption. This is again, in theory, a question prior to that of public-private division, since there is no necessity that a more substantive conception of distributive justice will be implemented through direct public provision of benefits: The level of public provision is logically secondary and can be determined, as we have said, only against the background of a solution to the distribution question.

IV. Redistribution

For substantively redistributive theories of justice this is problematic. It isn't clear how one can conceive of a utilitarian or Rawlsian distribution being carried out while the level of public provision is left unspecified. For the moment, however, let us put that issue aside and simply observe that many people would favor a frankly redistributive standard for social and economic justice, according to which libertarian procedural conditions do not suffice to confer justice on the outcome of economic transactions. These conceptions include (a) views that require additional procedural conditions, such as some positive form of equality of opportunity, through education, health care, child care support, etc.; (b) views that require a decent social minimum for its own sake; (c) utilitarian views that require transfer of resources from haves to have-nots because of the diminishing marginal utility of most possessions; (d) liberal egalitarian views like Rawls's, which combine equality of opportunity with priority to improvements in the condition of the worst off. We won't take up the merits of these views at this point but will concentrate on their relation to the issue of public-private division, which must now serve two purposes at once: distributive justice and the financing of public goods.

Redistribution need not take the form of public provision, but it may, and the choice between cash and in-kind redistributive transfers is important. But even if we set aside public provision that is specifically redistributive in intent, there will also be a consequence for the public provision of public goods, whose point is not redistributive. Their financing out of tax revenues will now also serve a redistributive purpose rather than mere efficiency, as in the earlier discussion. Distributive considerations will influence the allocation of the costs of public goods among taxpayers beyond the allocation of the surplus, already discussed. This has to be done even though we still rely mainly on efficiency, relative to a presumably just background distribution, in determining the appropriate *level* of public goods.

The abstract division of the process of justification into two stages is, we have said, problematic and highly artificial. (Where the distributive principle is utilitarian, it is particularly peculiar, because we will be piling one utilitarian argument on top of another.) However, suppose we can conceive of the solution to the distribution problem as logically prior, without specifying how it is to be implemented and without yet assuming anything about public provision. We would then have a basis for determining the efficient level of a public good such as defense, by comparison both with other public goods and with private expenditures. And having determined that, we would have determined the share of defense costs to be borne by different individuals, out of their different notional resources under the just distribution. Finally, we will be able to adjust their actual shares of the cost through taxes, as one way of creating that just distribution. This means that redistribution will usually take the form of a combination of direct transfers and differential contributions to the financing of public goods. But it is important to think of this as, in part, consisting of the support of public goods out of the resources of those who are benefited by redistribution.

Suppose Rich has a predistribution income of 100 and Poor has an income of 10, and that distributive justice would require a transfer from Rich to Poor of 10, leaving them with 90 and 20. Suppose that, relative to this just notional distribution, a level of spending on public goods to which Rich contributes 30% of 90 and Poor contributes 10% of 20 equalizes the marginal utility of public and private expenditures for both of them. This result can be achieved by taxing Rich 29 for the public goods budget and transferring another 8 from Rich to Poor.

V.   Transfer or Provision?

That still leaves the question of how best to implement redistribution apart from the financing of public goods. How should one decide between public provision and simple transfer of private resources? The question is further complicated by the fact that certain kinds of public provision may serve a double function, since they can be justified both as public goods and as forms of redistribution, and the actual reasons of their political supporters may be mixed. That is evident from the earlier discussion of the nondistributive efficiency arguments for a social minimum, universal education, health care, and so on. But in either case there seems something to be said for providing some of these things in kind, rather than doing it all in fungible cash. This doesn't have to take the form of public schools and colleges or public housing or a national health service: Some of it can be done with vouchers dedicated to certain purposes or with food stamps or housing allowances—thus preserving some of the efficiency advantages of market mechanisms of supply and allocation. But provision in kind seems justifiable for more than one reason.

The most important is that described by T. M. Scanlon in "Preference and Urgency."[6] Even if the reasons for helping those in need are frankly redistributive, the measure of value that is relied on by a conception of distributive justice ought to be itself objective enough to be accepted from the point of view of the diversity of value systems represented in the society. The satisfaction of individual preferences, whatever they might be, does not meet this standard. We may feel we owe each other the conditions of fair equality of opportunity, or a decent standard of living, but that does not mean we owe an individual help in obtaining something else instead, just because the individual values it even more.

In Scanlon's example, if someone would gladly forgo a decent diet in order to build a monument to his god, that doesn't mean that if we feel obliged to contribute to his getting enough to eat, we should also feel obliged to contribute an equivalent amount to the cost of his monument instead. Insofar as in-kind provision discourages such trade-offs and ensures that redistribution will be carried out in a common coin of value, it has an advantage over monetary redistribution. This holds even more clearly for the case where the reduction of socioeconomic inequality is also justified as a public good. The improvement in question has to be of value to everyone, and it is likely that specific benefits will more reliably produce the desired social effects.

There is also some reason for paternalism with regard to the meeting of basic needs: health, education, retirement, and insurance against disability and unemployment. It may be reasonable for the community not to trust individuals to be prudent in those respects, particularly if they don't have much money. For political purposes, it may be best to make such paternalistic programs universal in application, but their most important impact will be on those who don't have substantial extra private resources to provide a buffer against the effects of imprudence.

Still, it is hard to be confident about this question. It is possible that in the implementation of substantive redistribution, the line of public-private division should be drawn to leave the lion's share of distributed resources under private control, both for reasons of efficiency and to further values of autonomy. The familiar conservative rhetoric about people knowing better what to do with their money than the government does combines two claims: (1) that the money people earn before taxes is theirs, and they shouldn't be required to give it up for the benefit of others; (2) that whatever money is theirs, its management and expenditure is better left in their hands, to be controlled in accordance with their own values and judgments. The first point is antiredistributive; the second point is pro-autonomy. It is possible to accept some version of the second point without accepting the first. That is, one can maintain that it is best for people to decide individually what to do with "their" money, but at the same time affirm that government has a legitimate role, through design of the tax and property system, in determining what is "theirs"—what different individuals will end up with as disposable income and wealth, after taxes and transfers.

Pure resource distribution can be implemented by a substantial personal tax exemption, by a negative income tax (or earned income tax credit), by wage subsidies, by family allowances, or by a sizable demogrant that goes automatically to everyone. On the revenue side, distribution can be supported in various ways, of which progressive income taxation is only one. If there is a case against big government—against large public services and programs of public provision—it need not be a case against redistribution, which could in principle be carried out largely in cash, leaving people free to make their own private choices on how to use it: for health insurance, retirement annuities, and so forth. That would leave only public goods to be directly supplied by government programs, and their extent could be determined by efficiency considerations, provided a just distribution was assured.

All this leaves unaddressed the purely economic arguments against redistributive transfers, either in cash or in kind: arguments to the effect that they and the taxes needed to finance them have adverse consequences on investment, on work incentives for both high and low earners, on levels of employment and productivity—that the trickle-down effects of a hands-off policy are much better in actual outcome for the people one wants to help. Whatever may be the empirical merits of such claims (which we return to in chapter 6), they can provide arguments about tax justice only by reference to some standard of what makes one result more just than another. On some empirical assumptions, even a strongly egalitarian conception of justice like Rawls's difference principle cannot be implemented by redistribution from rich to poor, because the economic effects of such redistribution hurt the poor—for example, by leaving them with insufficient incentive to seek employment. If that were indeed the case, then the right distributive background would best be achieved by fewer transfers. This leaves in place the framework of justification that we have sketched for determining the correct level and financing of public goods relative to a conception of justice.

VI. Public Duties

Let us return finally to the special type of good mentioned earlier, which is neither a good for particular individuals in the society nor a public good for all of them, but rather a good in itself. If there are such things, we suggested, they might be justifiably supported by the state out of taxes under the heading of public duties rather than public goods. Examples would include foreign aid, support of the arts and sciences, and protection of endangered species. All these may have public and private good aspects as well, and foreign aid probably brings in some version of distributive justice on the global level, raising familiar and difficult questions about the interaction between international and domestic distributive justice.[7]

However, let us consider these things now in their aspect as goods that everyone has some obligation to promote if possible. One view would be that the fulfilment of this obligation should be left to individual choice, through private charity. But if one takes the other view, that the state may legitimately enforce such a contribution (against the background of a prior distribution of resources that is presumed not to be unjust), then the question will be how to decide what different people, at different economic levels, ought to be assessed for these purposes, and what the total contribution should be.

This question has a similar structure to the problem of public goods. The level of individual obligation generated by public duties will be a function not only of the importance of the good to be promoted or need to be met but also of the resources of the potential donor. Assigning the relevant values is obviously going to be a matter of moral and political disagreement, but it has to be done in some measure that allows comparison with both public and private goods. Support for the arts, famine relief for impoverished countries, national defense, and private goods, from housing to holidays, must all compete normatively for the marginal dollar.

The appropriate foreign aid budget will be the sum of the amounts that fulfill the obligations of the individual citizens, relative to the other possible employments of their individual resources. And if there is, in this case or in some other, a satiation point where less than this sum will suffice, then we are brought back to the question of how to divide the resulting moral "surplus." People in these circumstances would be required to give less than they could in principle be required to contribute to the purpose in question if the costs were higher. So the solution to the problem of financing the fulfilment of public duties fits into the same structure as the problem of public goods.

VII. Conclusion

Because the framework we have offered contains so many evaluative and empirical variables, it has no clear tax implications by itself. But it does imply that if we are favorable to the reduction of inequality or the provision of a decent minimum standard of living to all members of the society, we should distinguish this aim from any assumptions about the level of public provision and should also distinguish it from the independently desirable goal of financing public goods in such a way as to equalize the marginal utility of public and private outlays, for all individuals. Distribution and public-private division are distinct but richly interrelated issues. We have tried mainly to distinguish the factors that bear on their evaluation.

In summary, we would emphasize three points. First, there are substantial reasons quite apart from distributive justice for apportioning the cost of public expenditures unequally among those with unequal resources. Second, many more things than might initially seem to be public goods can plausibly be regarded as having a public good aspect and therefore are candidates for public provision without appealing to distributive justice. Third, if one accepts, as we and most other people do, a serious social requirement of distributive justice—even if only through the provision of a social minimum or the conditions of equal opportunity—then it is an open question whether this should be accomplished by transfer payments or by in-kind public provision or by vouchers dedicated to certain purposes but usable in the private market. It is compatible even with a strongly egalitarian conception of distributive justice that public provision should for practical reasons be mainly in the realm of public goods that benefit everyone, and that redistribution should be implemented not through public provision but mainly through transfer payments and differential tax assessment for the financing of public goods.

5

The Tax Base

I. Efficiency and Justice

What should be taxed? The issue of the choice of tax base has been prominent in the tax policy literature of recent decades, in large part because of a continuing controversy over whether the U.S. income tax should be replaced with a tax on consumption.[1] Since, on the standard definition, income comprises consumption plus increases in wealth, the debate here comes down to the theoretically and politically important question of the appropriate tax treatment of capital.[2]

As will be explained more fully in section III, the issue of income versus consumption taxation as the primary source of federal revenue is quite independent of the question of progressivity. When most people think of a consumption tax, they are likely to imagine a national sales tax, or perhaps a value-added tax, which is paid at the same rate by everyone—though it might be assessed at a higher rate on luxury goods and at a lower rate or not at all on essentials like food. But in fact, a consumption tax could have any degree of progressivity whatever, if, for example, it were designed just like the annual income tax, but with an exemption for all savings and investment until drawn down for consumption. Americans are already familiar with such exemptions in the form of IRAs and tax-exempt contributions to retirement plans. One way to implement a full consumption tax is simply to expand those exemptions to exclude all income that was not consumed.

This is not the only issue concerning the tax base to have received attention. Just as politically charged are various questions of exclusion that arise under both consumption and income bases—such as whether taxpayers should be allowed a deduction or credit for mortgage interest payments, health-care expenses, or charitable donations. At a more purely theoretical level, economists and philosophers have asked whether the ideal tax base should be people's opportunities or endowments—their potential as opposed to their actual consumption or income.

Most of the debate about the tax base, and the tax treatment of capital in particular, focuses on efficiency. Clearly, if two tax systems achieve the same aims (raising revenue for public provision, securing economic justice, perhaps providing certain desirable behavioral incentives), the system with lower costs is better. The most obvious costs of a tax scheme are those of administration, incurred both by the government and by taxpayers. In this connection some have argued that a consumption tax is simpler than an income tax and for that reason imposes lower administrative costs on individuals, businesses, and the tax collection bureaucracy.[3]

Less obvious, but well understood by economists, are the costs of tax "distortions." Distortions are undesired incentive effects from taxes, effects that in themselves carry a social cost by deterring choices that would produce social benefit. The most basic example, already mentioned in chapter 2, is the effect on the choice between labor and leisure caused by any consumption or income tax.[4] If the marginal tax rate applicable to an extra hour of work reduces the net benefit of the extra work to less than that of an extra hour of leisure, a rational worker will choose the leisure instead. As we shall see in the next chapter, the significance of this "substitution effect" in practice is unclear. But if it deters work, the tax harms both the worker and the potential employer, each of whom has lost the opportunity for gain—and benefits no one, since the work was not done and so no tax was collected.

As this example also shows, however, tax distortions in some form are unavoidable. The question is how to minimize them, consistently with the achievement of the aims of the system.[5] Here tax analysts have pointed out the great advantage of a "clean" or "broad" tax base, one with minimal exclusions and thus minimal tax distortion of investment and other market behavior.[6] One important possible reform would be the integration of the corporate and personal tax systems to eliminate the current tax preference for corporate debt over equity and the unwarranted disfavorable tax treatment of the corporate business form generally.[7] Along the same lines, it has been argued that either a pure income or a pure consumption base would be preferable to the current hybrid system, which taxes some but not all return to savings and thus distorts investment decisions.[8]

We take no stand on these important and contested efficiency issues. The question for this chapter is whether and in what ways the choice of tax base affects the justice, rather than the efficiency, of a government's economic institutions. Though we will consider the familiar categories of consumption, income, wealth, and endowment, together with the question of exclusions, our approach will be different in ways already marked in chapters 2 and 3.

II. Outcomes, not Burdens

Much of the argument of this chapter will be negative, rejecting arguments for and against the intrinsic fairness of one or another tax base. Our view is that the choice of tax base has only instrumental significance for economic justice. As we have said, a just tax scheme is one that finds its place in a set of economic institutions that together produce just and efficient social results. Since justice in taxation is not a matter of a fair distribution of tax burdens measured against a pretax baseline, it cannot be important in itself what pretax characteristics of taxpayers determine tax shares.

Thus, for example, an argument in favor of the income as opposed to the consumption base on the ground that capital accumulation affects ability to pay can be rejected for addressing the wrong question. The same goes for an argument that medical expenses should be deductible from an income or consumption base on the grounds that this kind of expenditure does not indicate a greater pretax level of welfare but rather the contrary.

In chapter 2 we argued that since the pretax distribution of welfare is both entirely imaginary and morally irrelevant it cannot matter whether a tax scheme imposes equal, proportional, or any other pattern of sacrifice as measured against that baseline. Unless one accepts a libertarian conception of private property, it does not matter whether the tax base is more or less accurate at capturing people's pretax "ability to pay" or levels of welfare. And if a particular tax base leads to a different relative standing of individuals compared to the hypothetical pretax situation, this does not in itself pose any problem of horizontal equity.

Once we reject the idea that justice in taxation is a matter of ensuring a fair distribution of tax burdens relative to the pretax baseline, the issue of the tax base does not disappear, but it takes on a purely instrumental significance as far as justice is concerned: Different tax bases may be better or worse suited to the tax system's task of helping to secure just social outcomes. The criteria for instrumental success obviously depend upon the criteria for social justice, but the relation may not be simple. If, for example, justice requires special attention to the welfare of the worst off, and if we think consumption is a pretty good measure of welfare, it doesn't follow that consumption is the right tax base. Income may be better as a tax base if it is more effective in its distributive effects on consumption.

We begin, however, by reviewing the fairness-based arguments that have been made about the choice of tax base.

III. The Consumption Base and Fairness to Savers

There are many varieties of consumption tax, the most familiar to Americans being state and local retail sales taxes. Functionally equivalent is the Value-Added Tax (VAT) familiar to Europeans and Canadians (as the Goods and Services Tax) and recently introduced in Australia amid intense partisan political controversy (the opposition Labor Party pledged to "roll back" the tax upon regaining government on the ground that it is unfair to lower-income people). In all these cases, of course, the sales tax or VAT does not stand alone but rather supplements an income tax. In the current radical tax policy climate in the United States, however, there have been several apparently serious congressional proposals to abolish the income tax entirely and replace it with a federal retail sales tax.[9] These proposals include a suggestion for a rebate to low income earners to offset the extreme regressivity of taxing everyone a fixed amount on the consumption dollar.*

More seriously in contention is the so-called flat tax proposal of Robert Hall and Alvin Rabushka, which is currently championed in Congress by House Majority Leader Dick Armey[10] and was a centerpiece of Steve Forbes's lavishly self-funded presidential campaigns in 1996 and 2000. This scheme is essentially a VAT with wages taken out of the business tax base and taxed instead at the level of individuals.[11] The label "flat" seems deliberately misleading, since it is used to suggest a flat or proportionate average rate. Hall and Rabushka write that the "principle of equity embodied in the flat tax is that every taxpayer pays taxes in direct proportion to his income."[12] In fact, however, the proposal includes a personal exemption to individuals' taxable income, so even though there is only one (nonzero) tax rate (19%) the result is a progressive scheme, as the authors themselves point out.[13]

Indeed, the whole point of taking wages out of the business tax base and collecting tax from individual workers is to allow for progression[14]—without the need for a rebate, or some kind of electronic card that keeps track of purchases, as economist Laurence Kotlikoff has proposed for a sales tax system.[15] A potentially more progressive variation is what David Bradford calls the X tax, in which there is not only a personal exemption but also graduated rates.[16] As this brief

---

*Though these proposals may not be taken terribly seriously, they cannot be ignored. With such views in the air, the flat tax can seem like a sensible, moderate position.

discussion makes clear, the distinct issues of progression, graduated rates, and choice of tax base tend to be run together in the current debate.[17]

A quite different way of implementing a consumption base is via a cash-flow or expenditure tax. This approach is defended in Nicholas Kaldor's widely influential 1955 book, *An Expenditure Tax*,[18] and has been much discussed by legal theorists since William Andrews's 1974 article, "A Consumption-Type or Cash Flow Personal Income Tax." Along with the retail sales tax, the cash flow tax is the approach most naturally suggested by the concept of consumption, since under this scheme people are literally taxed on their consumption or expenditure: individuals pay tax on all their earnings but deduct any amounts saved in the tax year. Since money dissaved and spent is consumption, withdrawals from savings and borrowings are included in the tax base. A scheme of this kind has been proposed in the U.S. Congress by Senators Sam Nunn and Pete Domenici under the label USA Tax (for Unlimited Savings Allowance).[19]

Compared to the cash-flow tax, it is not as easy to see why the "flat tax" or X tax are consumption taxes. This follows from two facts. First, as in a standard VAT, businesses immediately deduct ("expense") the cost of machinery and other durable goods rather than claiming depreciation allowances over time, as is the case under an income tax.[20] Expensing is, in effect, a deduction for saving. Second, the tax on individuals is on wages only: all returns to capital—dividends, interest, capital gains—are exempt. Generally speaking, if the rates are constant, a tax that allows a deduction for savings or investment and one that exempts the return to savings or investment are financially equivalent.[21]

This equivalence allows us to say, furthermore, that any consumption tax scheme, in taxing not accretions to wealth as such, but rather only consumption, exempts from taxation normal returns to investment.[22] This is why a consumption tax is said to be neutral with respect to the choice between saving and current consumption—the existence of the tax does not change the value of either option. It is on this point that much of the controversy over the fairness of consumption versus income taxes hinges.

Suppose that Kurt has $100 in wage income to either spend immediately or invest at 10%. If taxes are left out of account, his choice is between $100 now and $110 a year from now. Under an income tax, at a marginal rate of 50%, his choice is between $50 now and $52.50 next year—a return of only 5%, since he pays tax on the interest earned as well as his wages. Depending on Kurt's "discount rate"—the percentage return that he regards as sufficient to make it worthwhile to postpone consumption for a year—the halving of the percentage return to investment caused by the tax may affect his choice. If so, we see here the substitution effect of a tax on capital income: the tax leads Kurt to substitute current consumption for savings. But unlike the substitution effect on the choice between labor and leisure, there is something a tax system can realistically do to avoid this "distortion"—exempt capital income from tax, thus making the system tax-neutral between savings and consumption.

An instrumental reason why this might seem desirable is that we regard more investment as good for economic growth. To the extent that this is so, a tax system should, all else being equal, attempt to encourage rather than discourage savings. The available empirical evidence, however, suggests that savings behavior is rather unresponsive to changes in the after-tax rate of return.[23] Thus, this purely instrumental argument for a consumption base appears to fail.

But an independent claim of equity is very often made in this connection, which we particularly want to examine.[24] Let us imagine that Kurt chooses to save for a year, despite the 50% tax on his return.[25] Compare now Bert, who has the same income and wealth, but who would not choose to save at 10% even if his yield were exempt from tax. Unlike Kurt, Bert is not at all affected by the tax on capital income. That the income tax imposes a cost on Kurt but not Bert, just because of Kurt's preference for saving, is said to be unfair.[26] When the point is presented as starkly as this, it is rather puzzling. As Musgrave notes, it seems to presuppose rather than argue for the claim that consumption rather than income is the appropriate tax base.[27] For, of course, if fair taxation taxes returns to saving, it is unfair not to do so.

What we have here is a horizontal equity argument: Bert

and Kurt are thought to be, in some relevant sense, identically situated in the no-tax world, but they are treated unequally by the income tax. We have explained in earlier chapters why the idea of the "no-tax world" is incoherent. But in order to examine the argument, let us suppose that the idea of a world in which everyone has full disposal of their pretax resources makes sense.

Since what is in question is precisely the tax base, the claimed inequity of a tax on income must arise on a basis for comparison other than income or consumption. Welfare might seem to be the natural candidate, but it actually will not do. For even if Kurt and Bert are identically situated in terms of income and wealth, we cannot say that they are equally well off in the no-tax world, either this year or in the long run. What we know is that given Bert's discount rate it is not worthwhile for him to save, even without taxes, while the opposite is true for Kurt. This tells us nothing about Kurt's and Bert's relative levels of welfare—neither that they are the same nor that they are different.[28]

But suppose we simply assume that Kurt and Bert, with equal income and wealth, are roughly equally well-off in the no-tax world, in spite of the difference in their discount rates. Even so, the argument that they should be taxed the same so that this equality is preserved obviously runs afoul of our fundamental point that there is no ground for treating the pretax distribution of welfare as an ethically significant baseline. But to test this point it is worth pursuing the "fairness to savers" argument further, since in its best version it derives from a theory of justice that may seem to make sense of that baseline after all. The following evaluation of the fairness to savers argument therefore continues the discussion of whether there is any plausible theory of justice that has a place for the traditional criteria of tax equity.

IV. Fairness as Equal Liberty

In Bradford's influential presentation of the fairness to savers argument, the explicit premise is that taxation ought not to change the values of the opportunities or options that savers and current spenders have in the no-tax world.[29] In other words, if the (hypothetical, no-government) market has favored Kurt's preferences rather than Bert's, by making available a savings option that he would choose, then tax burdens should not disturb that advantage and make the actual world relatively less favorable to Kurt. More accurately, the claim is that so long as two people such as Kurt and Bert are equals in that, with the same income and wealth, they face equal opportunities to consume and to save, horizontal equity requires that the one should not be burdened by taxes more than the other. As Bradford makes clear, this argument is not specific to preferences over saving; it would be equally unjust, on this line of thought, to tax food more heavily than clothing, thus penalizing those who prefer to eat well relative to those who prefer to dress well.[30]

Clearly, the baseline of pretax market outcomes is given moral significance here, since it is only if relative market prices for food and clothing are, in some sense, what they should be, that it could be unfair to anyone to alter them through taxation. Instead of the view that the distribution of welfare produced by the market is presumptively just, Bradford's view is that the relative pricing of the range of opportunities produced by the market is presumptively just. Or rather, he presumes that this would be so if everyone had equal resources to take advantage of those opportunities.*

This crucial assumption of equal resources suggests an egalitarian market-based view of justice very like that of Ronald Dworkin.[31] Both the foundations and details of Dworkin's view are complex, but its clear implication is that an egalitarian market world, one where people start out life with equal holdings of financial *and* human capital, is just, whatever the resulting distribution of welfare. If one person prefers more expensive food or clothing than another,

---

*Richard Epstein embraces this principle of "tax neutrality" without the stipulation of equal resources. "The ideal of tax neutrality simply provides that the system of taxation, as far as possible, should preserve the relative priorities that individuals attach to various activities. The function of the state is to protect liberty and property. It is not to aid one group or another in skewing the uses to which individuals put their natural endowments" (Epstein 1987, 55).

this may affect their relative welfare, but it isn't unfair. In such a world we can say that what people get is a function purely of factors for which they are responsible and so there is no warrant for redistribution by the state.[32] In particular, if Bert ends up less well off than Kurt in the egalitarian market world because of his aversion to saving, that is his lookout. Likewise, if a full-time surfer who started out with the same resources is now much worse off than either of them because of his aversion to gainful employment, he has only himself to blame for the effects of his decisions.

Without claiming that either Bradford or Dworkin would acknowledge this rough account, let us call the view under discussion *equal libertarianism*. It is egalitarian because it insists on equality of initial resource holdings, libertarian because it treats market outcomes that result from such equal starting places as presumptively just. While the moral outlook behind this view could be that the ideal market gives people the rewards they deserve, it is usually understood as an entitlement-based theory. There is no injustice in a market world where everyone starts out with the same resources—even if that world ends up very unequal, with successful lawyers much better-off than unsuccessful poets, and some destitution—because what people ought to get depends on the choices they have made. In other words, given a truly equal starting point, people cannot complain of their market rewards when those rewards result from their free choices in the context of the equally free choices of others, likewise expressed through the market. Whether this market-based standard of responsibility needs to be justified at a deeper level in terms of desert, or the extent to which the individual's choices have satisfied the collective preferences of others, is a question we leave aside.[33]

One apparent implication of this view is that the ideal tax base would be endowment. Bradford explicitly embraces this conclusion: ideally, the surfer would be taxed the same as Bert and Kurt, since they all had the same lifetime opportunities.[34] We discuss endowment taxation separately in section VIII.

Although we don't believe that this conception of justice is correct, because it gives too much weight to individual responsibility, we won't pursue that disagreement here. The point we want to make is rather that, even if the basic moral idea is accepted, equal libertarianism does not, in the end, provide support for the fairness to savers argument; nor does it threaten our rejection of the use of a baseline of pretax market outcomes in the theory of tax justice.

The fairness-to-savers argument is supposed to go like this. There is a general claim that so long as people start life with equal wealth and human capital, they should bear the same tax burden as measured against pretax market outcomes. And then it is offered as a particular implication of this claim that no one should bear a higher tax burden than another just because of a relatively stronger preference for saving over current consumption. If the general claim were right, it might seem to amount to a direct refutation of our position that justice in taxation is not a matter of extracting equal (or any other distribution of) sacrifice as measured against a pretax baseline. But this does not follow for the simple reason that, in the absence of government, people do not start life with equal financial and human capital.

To create a just equal libertarian society, the state would have to take giant steps to ensure equality of initial resources.[35] Partly, this could be done by redistributing property rights in financial wealth and providing free education (necessary since children presumably cannot be held responsible for their parents' spending choices). But when it comes to those aspects of human capital that are provided unequally by nature, the state cannot literally make us all equal. Rather, it must, via the tax and transfer system, compensate those who are less lucky in what Rawls calls "the natural lottery." Compensation through tax and transfer would also be required if the public education system does not, in fact, equalize opportunities for all those similarly talented and motivated, which is likely to be the case in any actual world we can imagine.

In short, no actual pretax distribution is the result of equal resources employed in the exercise of equal opportunities, and justice in taxation cannot simply be a matter of imposing equal burdens as measured against such a baseline. Taxation is a necessary part of the set of state institutions that would be needed, on the equal libertarian theory, to create the preconditions for a market in which whatever happens is just.[36] Anything remotely resembling the equal libertarian ideal could only be created in a *post*-tax world. Since that is so, there remains no separate question of tax justice, to which the principle of equal sacrifice relative to pretax outcomes could provide the answer.

Equal libertarianism does, however, make sense of a much more limited use of the principle of equal sacrifice. We argued in chapter 4 that the problem of raising revenue for public goods is theoretically distinct from the problem of distribution, despite the fact that these two functions of taxation are intertwined in practice. The approach we endorsed was to assume a hypothetical just distribution and determine an efficient allocation of public goods from that baseline. The same basic approach is available to the equal libertarian: a hypothetical equal distribution of resources could serve as the baseline for the application of equal sacrifice as a criterion for justice in the funding of public goods. This is not, of course, the rehabilitation of the principle of equal sacrifice as a general principle of tax justice. The baseline used is not pretax outcomes but rather a hypothetical ideal distribution of resources, and the scope of the principle is limited to but one of the functions of taxation.

Moreover, this limited possible role for the principle of equal sacrifice is not sufficient to sustain the fairness to savers argument. Even if we lived in a society where government institutions did manage to bring about equal starting places, it could not be said that an income tax would unfairly alter the value of opportunities in that hypothetical just world. As we will see in section VII, there is no reason in justice to rule out income taxation as part of the best means to equal starting places. So the most that could be said is that it would be unfair to use an income tax for that part of the tax burden that is earmarked for the funding of public goods rather than for redistribution. Apart from the fact that it is hard to see how this conclusion could be put into practice, the now very limited scope of the charge of unfairness considerably weakens its force.

In any event, we do not live in the equal libertarian's ideal market society or in a society that shows any sign of trying to achieve that ideal through its economic institutions. And so long as we do not, we cannot argue about the tax base under the pretense that the opportunities presented in our actual, inegalitarian, market world are just and thus not to be disturbed through taxation. The fairness-to-savers argument as here reconstructed gets off the ground only in the equal libertarian's utopia.

There are two further reasons to reject the fairness-to-savers argument. First, the argument as presented would condemn taxation of wage income for the very same reason that it condemns taxation of capital income. A consumption tax strives to be fair to savers (versus spenders) but is unfair to workers because it penalizes those who prefer work with more consumption over leisure with less. As Barbara Fried notes, it is hard to see any fairness rationale at all for this hybrid approach.[37] It is true that the only way to avoid the supposed unfairness to workers is to impose a lump-sum tax—either a head tax, the same amount for everyone, or an endowment tax, a fixed amount for each person based on potential earnings. Neither option is remotely plausible. But if fairness to workers is not possible for this reason, there is no reason to think that overall fairness is nevertheless advanced by insisting on fairness to savers. Removing but one kind of unfairness in a multiply unfair world might make things less fair, overall.

Second, as we saw in chapter 2, the tax system is not the only means by which government affects the relative values of various options presented by a market. Interest rate regulation affects the return to savings, transportation policy affects the relative value of different investment options.[38] Thus, even if equality of opportunity were somehow given as part of our natural world and so did not have to be secured by means of government institutions, the idea of a no-government market world that could be used as a baseline for fairness in government economic policy would remain a fantasy.

After going through all these reasons to reject the fairness-to-savers argument you may still feel the force of the initial intuition: Isn't it *obviously* unfair to tax food more heavily than clothes, thus disadvantaging food lovers relative to clothes lovers? And if so, why isn't the same concern due to savers? But the considerations just advanced show that it would not be in itself unfair to tax food more heavily than clothes. The thought that it would be supposes an imaginary market in which relative prices for food and clothes are as they should be. Of course, an entirely arbitrary decision to tax some consumption choices more heavily than others would be suspect, indicating, perhaps, unwarranted favoritism for a specific industry. But if the differential tax treatment were justified by respectable social goals (an unlikely possibility in this case), it would be perfectly legitimate from the point of view of justice.

Similarly, the pretax return to savings, and hence the relative pretax cost of choosing immediate rather than future consumption, has no presumptive correctness as the result of an ideal capital market. So there is nothing unfair, per se, in a tax that affects the relation between those costs. Whether it is justified will depend on its other consequences.

V. Desert and the Accumulation of Capital: The "Common Pool"

However, there is still another venerable claim of fairness on behalf of the consumption tax that has to be dealt with. Nicholas Kaldor wrote that a consumption tax is preferable to an income tax since it "would tax people according to the amount which they take out of the common pool, and not according to what they put into it."[39] This distinct ethical argument for the consumption base has been quite influential.[40] Kaldor is not just making the instrumental claim that the consumption base encourages savings. Rather, his claim is that *since* saving is socially beneficial, it is not fair to tax savers more heavily.

There are obvious objections to be made to Kaldor's language: a person's wealth does contribute to the social good so long as it is productively invested, but this does not make it part of a common pool—as many have pointed out, it remains securely in the private pool of its owner.[41] It may be used for productive purposes, but it stays under private control. Furthermore, it is inaccurate to describe consumption as taking things out of the common pool—as if the quantity of consumables were fixed and someone who bought a shirt or a sandwich left fewer shirts and sandwiches for everybody else. Consumption stimulates production and is as essential for the growth of the social product as is investment.

A slightly more plausible interpretation of the argument is this. Investment contributes to the social good by making private resources available for production and should therefore be both encouraged and rewarded. Even if a consumption tax does not in practice lead to greater rates of savings than an income tax, it is preferable on ethical grounds just because it does not penalize those who choose to save. Saving benefits society, and it isn't right to tax "praiseworthy"[42] activities *more*.

We have here a desert argument for the consumption base, appealing not to the idea that markets reward desert and so provide a baseline for a horizontal equity claim, but rather to the very different idea that as between savers and current spenders, the former deserve to be better off, or at any rate not worse off. The fairness-to-savers argument proceeds on the assumption that the tax code should not penalize savers for what is after all just a consumption choice. The common pool argument, by contrast, insists that some consumption choices are more praiseworthy than others, and the tax code should reflect this fact.

The moralization of the accumulation of capital has an illustrious history. Here is Adam Smith on the topic.

> By what a frugal man annually saves, he not only affords maintenance of an additional number of productive hands, for that or the ensuing year, but like the founder of a public workhouse, he establishes as it were a perpetual fund for the maintenance of an equal number in all times to come. . . . The prodigal perverts [this fund]. . . . By not confining his expence within his income, he encroaches on his capital. Like him who perverts the revenues of some pious foundation to profane purposes, he pays the wages of idleness with those

funds which the frugality of his forefather had, as it were, consecrated to the maintenance of industry.[43]

Smith did not, however, argue from the superior virtue of the frugal to the superiority of the consumption base.

Even if we agree that savers are morally superior to spenders, the argument from this moral judgment to the consumption base is unpersuasive. There can be no justice in linking taxation to some aspects of moral desert but not to others, and there are plenty of other ways to be virtuous than by accumulating capital. Indeed, the very same capitalist moral ideal of frugal industry implies that the hardworking should not be taxed more than the indolent. But of course that occurs under a consumption tax just as surely as under an income tax, since the indolent, having less income, will also consume less.

The general point here is that tax policy cannot be evaluated by piecemeal intuitions of desert. If what people deserve is relevant to tax design, that can only be because it is relevant to social justice; it has to depend on a desert-based theory of justice and a full account of the implications of that theory for the totality of economic institutions. The common pool argument for the consumption base is a classic example of the narrowness of focus that bedevils tax theory.

A final historical note: Kaldor attributes the common pool argument to Hobbes, citing these sentences from *Leviathan*:

> [T]he Equality of Imposition, consisteth rather in the Equality of that which is consumed, than of the riches of the person that consume the same. For what reason is there, that he which laboureth much, and sparing the fruits of his labour, consumeth little, should be more charged, than he that living idly, getteth little, and spendeth all he gets; seeing the one hath no more protection from the Common-wealth, then the other? But when the Impositions, are layd upon those things which men consume, every man payeth equally for what he useth: Nor is the Common-wealth defrauded, by the luxurious waste of private men.[44]

Though many have followed Kaldor's attribution, this passage does not support the common pool idea, or any other desert-based reason for choosing the consumption base. In the last quoted sentence, Hobbes seems to suggest that an income base will encourage waste, rather than savings; this is the purely instrumental argument in favor of the consumption base. The rest of the quotation needs to be read in context. Immediately prior to this passage, Hobbes announces the benefit principle of tax justice. His defense of the consumption tax base is therefore most plausibly read as an argument that consumption is a better measure of the benefit someone receives from the protection of the state than is income.

That brings us to our next topic: To what extent does the accumulation of capital in itself increase a person's welfare? And does this provide an argument for income rather than consumption as the tax base?

VI. Wealth and Welfare

Opponents of the consumption base sometimes argue that since people with high incomes consume a lower proportion of their income than those with low incomes, the consumption base is objectionably regressive.[45] Here we have a vertical equity argument. As with the horizontal equity argument in favor of the consumption base, this argument is question-begging if it simply assumes that income is the right metric for comparison. So we must interpret the argument as follows: accretions to wealth, not just consumption, add to welfare; therefore, replacing an income tax with a consumption tax would reduce the tax burden on those with high levels of welfare at the expense of the worse off.

As Bradford notes, the most this argument really shows is that it would be regressive to replace an income tax with a consumption tax at the same rates.[46] If the proportion of income consumed decreases with increasing income, a more progressive rate structure under a consumption tax should be able to preserve whatever distribution of burdens a given income tax scheme imposed.

There are two ways in which the argument could be rephrased. First, it could be claimed that the regressive effect is not so easily avoided in practice. If, in order to maintain revenue and achieve the desired level of progressivity the graduated rates under a consumption tax would rise so high as to scare off legislators then, as a practical matter, any shift to a consumption tax would indeed turn out to be regressive. This is potentially a very important concern; we discuss similar practical political considerations in chapter 9.

Second, the claim could be narrowed: considering two people with different incomes but the same level of consumption,* it could be said that a consumption tax fails to achieve vertical equity because it imposes the same tax on people who are not equally well-off.[47] Since, as we have said repeatedly, justice in taxation is not a matter of securing a particular distribution of tax burdens as against a pretax distribution of welfare but depends rather on promoting a just overall outcome, even this narrow claim must be rejected. But there remains an important underlying concern. So long as levels of welfare are relevant to justice in social outcomes, it will matter whether wealth affects human welfare. The choice of tax base must be sensitive to its effect on the distribution of wealth in the outcome, if wealth produces something that is important for social justice.

Most theories of distributive justice are concerned with how well off people are, both absolutely and relatively. They hold that welfare matters, and that certain kinds of inequality in its distribution are undesirable. While some components of welfare—such as health, education, leisure, and longevity—can be measured directly, many must be guessed at by measuring the means to their achievement—means such as income, consumption, and wealth.

But the problem is not just one of measurement. As we saw in chapters 3 and 4, while economic policy must make use of some metric to evaluate the effects of different institutional arrangements on the quality of people's lives, there is no

---

*This could be true even taking whole lives as the proper basis for comparison (see chapter 7, section IV): It should not be assumed that the higher income person will consume all income and wealth before death.

single account of welfare that everyone accepts. How should a government react if people claim that while publicly funded health care does not make their lives go better, a new monument to their god would?

One option is to proceed on a fully worked out and inevitably controversial theory of the human good. Another is to abstract from disagreement about the components of welfare so far as this is possible; thus, Rawls advocates a metric of "primary social goods," which include income and wealth, understood to be all-purpose means that are required for the pursuit of any conception of the good. Neither option is without its serious problems; no doubt the best solution lies somewhere in between. We cannot do justice to the complex problem of the metric here, but we should note that the right question with regard to wealth is not, "Does wealth, on the best theory of welfare, help make a person's life go better?" but rather, "Does wealth find a place in the most appropriate metric for the collective political assessment of social outcomes?" This suggests that the metric used should be as uncontroversial as possible.

It is rightly taken for granted by almost everyone that explicit (i.e., paid-for) *consumption* will be part of the best metric. On most accounts of welfare, it is at least roughly true that the more money people spend on goods and services (taking into account the diminishing value of each additional dollar's worth), the better off they are. But it should be obvious that wealth is an independent source of welfare, quite apart from the fact that some of it may be consumed later. As Henry Simons famously put it, in 1938, "In a world where capital accumulation proceeds as it does now, there is something sadly inadequate about the idea of saving as postponed consumption."[48] Commentators typically mention such factors as security, political power, and social standing.[49]

Even if it is never consumed, wealth contributes to a person's welfare because it is known to be available should personal economic disaster strike—perhaps in the form of unemployment or a medical emergency for which available health insurance is inadequate. The current trend in the United States and elsewhere of dismantling government safety nets makes the importance of wealth as security all the more obvious.

Wealth leads to political power in the United States, since the possibility of significant contribution to a politician's funds encourages special treatment. But this is important less from the point of view of welfare than from the point of view of the democratic process, whose corruption by great disparities of wealth was pointed out already by Aristotle in the fourth century B.C.[50] Whether wealth should be a target of taxes for this reason is doubtful, since effective control of campaign financing would seem to be the preferable remedy.

For some people being wealthy is desirable independently of the security factor. The satisfaction many people derive from wealth is essentially comparative;[51] indeed, the very idea of being wealthy is comparative. So "social standing" is a plausible description of one aspect of wealth's contribution to welfare, and by the same token, poverty reduces welfare through the awareness of relative deprivation, in addition to its strictly material disadvantages.

Even though the incentive effects may be economically useful, there is something regrettable about the extent to which these purely comparative concerns motivate us, particularly those who are not poor. Perhaps the whole phenomenon is irrational and the very wealthy are not significantly better off just for having more capital. Yet, relative disadvantage in social standing does produce a real harm for those with very few possessions—a kind of stigma. A proper treatment of this issue would require serious discussion of the general phenomenon of social class; though we cannot pursue that topic here, we can say that the contribution of inequalities in wealth to social standing will be reflected in a reasonable metric of welfare. The contribution of very unequal levels of consumption to social standing is even more obvious,[52] but wealth clearly plays an independent role.

One argument on the other side needs to be answered—an argument that savings and wealth are subsidiary to consumption and derive their value entirely from it. Typically, people borrow when young, save in their highest-earning middle years, and dissave when old. One evident purpose of saving is thus to smooth out consumption over the course of a person's life.[53] Some economists have asserted that all capital accumulation can be explained in this way, which would mean that any wealth left over at death would be due to the impossibility of predicting the time of death with certainty (if this could be done, even wealth kept as security should in principle be used up in a last great consumption binge—though if the wealth is substantial the binge might merely hasten one's demise).

But this extreme "life cycle model" of savings cannot explain the phenomenon of very large bequests or the apparent lack of demand for annuity insurance.[54] Economists disagree greatly in their estimates of the percentage of capital accumulation in the United States that is due to gifts or bequests, but estimates average out to about 50%.[55] Despite some fanatical attempts to explain all such transfers in terms of the narrow self-interest of the accumulator of the wealth (invoking the idea of an implicit quid pro quo between parents and children), it is not credible to rule out the simple and obvious motive of benefit to family members. This is hardly an irrational preference. Having the ability to benefit people one loves is a good for the donor as well as the recipient—a further aspect of the contribution of wealth to welfare. Clearly, the impact of wealth on a person's security, social status, and ability to benefit family members should be recognized by a reasonable metric for the assessment of social outcomes.*

Relative levels of wealth could, in principle, be adjusted through other aspects of the legal system, but the most efficient means is surely the tax code.[56] The upshot of the connection between wealth and welfare is thus that, for theories that regard significant inequalities as prima facie undesirable, a consumption tax standing alone will, other things equal, be an inferior means of promoting distributive justice, because it will favor the unequal accumulation of wealth.

This leaves open the question whether the superior alternative is an income tax or a consumption tax coupled with

---

*However, this particular contribution can be addressed directly by separate wealth-transfer taxation, or by counting transfers as a form of consumption by the donor—an issue we defer until chapter 7.

an annual wealth tax. That, however, is a purely pragmatic question, since an income tax and a wealth tax are roughly equivalent as far as the taxation of capital is concerned. An annual tax on the value of an asset can be roughly duplicated by an annual tax, at a higher rate, on the income that asset produces.[57] So the question to ask about the choice between an income tax and a consumption plus wealth tax is whether one is more efficient than another, all things considered.[58] As with the other difficult questions of implementation raised by the taxation of capital—such as the realization requirement and the separate corporate income tax scheme—we take no stand.

We now turn to a quite different problem about the implementation of a tax on capital accumulation. It turns out that the ability of an income or wealth tax scheme to burden normal returns to financial capital is limited, in theory at least, to accumulation comprising the "return to waiting"—the risk-free rate of return. The reason is that, due to the deductibility of capital losses under either an income or a wealth tax, investors can, whatever the tax rate, reallocate their portfolios so that the expected after-tax rate of return is reduced only by the equivalent of the tax on the risk-free rate of return for the full investment.[59]

Leaving aside for now the extent to which this theoretical point applies to actual tax codes and actual investors, its potential implication is important, since the real (inflation adjusted) risk-free rate of return has historically been very low—under 1% since the 1940s in the United States.[60] This is not the route to grand fortunes, and it is understandable that many advocates of the consumption tax argue that even if wealth should, in principle, be taxed, the minor difference between the income and consumption bases in this respect cannot provide a strong argument in favor of the former.[61]

This question cannot be answered, however, by considering only the direct impact of income tax on the accumulation of wealth. An income tax promotes justice not only by the distribution of tax burdens but also by raising revenue—which can, of course, be used for redistributive purposes. Even though investors can avoid a reduction in their rate of return greater than the tax on the risk-free rate, that doesn't mean that the return to risk escapes tax.

In order to avoid a tax burden on the return to risk, the investor simply has to increase the riskiness of the portfolio. Because of the deductibility of losses, the government shares that increased risk, which means that as a result of the reallocation, although the investor's expected after-tax return stays near what it would have been in the absence of the tax, the expected pretax return goes up, and therefore the expected tax revenue also goes up—though also with greater risk. The government is made a partner in a risky investment, and the desirability of this consequence of income taxation is part of the issue. Is it a bad thing that such taxation (a) does not effectively inhibit accumulation of wealth through the return to risk (historically the major source of wealth), (b) encourages an increase in the riskiness of investments, (c) makes tax revenue dependent on those more risky returns?

The answers to these questions are not obvious. As Bankman and Griffith put it, "The desirability of taxing risk premia cannot be determined without a more adequate theory of how government spreads its risk back among its citizens."[62] This seems to us another example of a question that is in danger of being addressed from too narrow a focus—namely, the immediate impact of the tax on taxpayers. It is important to place such a tax in a larger context, including how the revenue will be used. Tax revenue on the return to risk has played a role in generating the recent federal surpluses, because of profits from the stock market boom. Since economic predictions are inexact, there is inevitably significant risk in the tax base in any case. Whether the risk is unacceptably elevated by the effects on taxpayer behavior of deductibility of investment losses under the income tax depends on how this translates into consequences for those who are the beneficiaries of government activities that will have to be curtailed if the risk goes bad.

Still, we seem to be faced with the problem that, while tax revenues can be realized from the accumulation of wealth, income and wealth taxes cannot consistently limit the accumulation of wealth that comes from the return to risk, its main source.[63] As we discuss in chapter 7, wealth transfer taxation can reach wealth accumulated through gratuitous receipts, as can inclusion of such receipts in the tax base of donees; but that is obviously only a partial solution. How much does this limit to the feasible taxation of wealth matter, from the point of view of justice?

That depends in part on the contribution wealth-based security and social standing make to a person's welfare, and also on the extent to which purely comparative differences in wealth diminish the welfare of those who have less. On the whole, we believe justice should be more concerned with raising the absolute level of people with few resources than with reducing inequalities from the top. So if income or wealth taxation generates revenue that is used for the former purpose, it may not matter so much if it doesn't also promote the latter.

A final note. The best metric for the assessment of social outcomes may count possession of a given amount of wealth as making either a greater or lesser contribution to welfare than its consumption. (There is no reason of justice, then, to think that wealth and consumption taxation must be related as they are in an income tax with a single rate applied to all forms of income.[64]) And the relationship may well vary, depending on levels of consumption and wealth. Thus, it seems quite likely that an extra few million dollars in a CEO's or star basketball player's salary will matter rather little in virtue of the extra goods and services it can buy. And as far as social standing is concerned, it may be that at this level wealth matters more than consumption: After a certain point, even observers of the consumption of others fail to notice the difference, but everyone can understand the difference between 100 and 200 million dollars in net worth.[65]

VII. Wealth and Opportunity

According to equal libertarianism, justice consists in equality of opportunity in a market economy—where equality of opportunity means equality of all factors that may affect market returns but for which a person is not responsible. There are also other, more limited versions of equality of opportunity as a principle of justice. One is the view that opportunities must be equal only in the negative sense that no person is arbitrarily excluded from a career or from economic interaction on such grounds as race, sex, or religion. This is the traditional liberal principle of "careers open to talents."

Significantly more egalitarian than this is the principle that Rawls calls "fair equality of opportunity," which insists not only on the absence of arbitrary barriers but also on equality of initial chances for those with comparable talents, ensured through provision of an equal material and educational starting point—a level playing field for those setting out in life. But this standard still accepts differential rewards due to different natural talents.

"Careers open to talents" is, in fact, just a minor modification of full-fledged libertarianism. It is a weak form of equal opportunity that implies radical and persistent inequality of results, if used as the sole standard of distributive justice—results that almost no one today would accept. By contrast, equal libertarianism and fair equality of opportunity embody much more substantial ideals of equal chances for the members of a society.[66]

For these theories of justice, the importance of wealth comes not from its contribution to welfare but from its role in determining people's opportunities in life. Evidently, those with wealth have greater opportunity to pursue their interests in a capitalist economy than those without. Literal equality of opportunity would require that wealth should be equal at the start of (adult) life and that opportunities for the accumulation of wealth should be equal over the course of life. If this condition of justice is given high priority, the implication for wealth transfer is radical: Setting aside the inevitable practical obstacles to such a policy, the prima facie ideal would be that gifts should be strictly limited and estates redistributed among the general population, so that everyone had the same start in life. We return to this issue in chapter 7.

The implication for the taxation of wealth accumulated from the investment of earnings is different. If people really did start out with the same financial assets and educational benefits, then, ignoring gifts and bequests, the theory of fair equality of opportunity would actually require no taxation for the purpose of adjusting market returns—neither of wealth nor of consumption. A considerable amount of redistributive taxation would nevertheless be needed in order to provide equal education and training for all.

Equal libertarianism, by contrast, would require additional redistribution in order to compensate for differential market returns due to differences in natural talents. But there seems to be no reason in justice, on these theories, either to include or to exclude wealth in the base of such taxation. Since they hold that without the relevant kind of equality of opportunity the prevailing distributions of consumption, income, and wealth are not just, there is no principled ground for taxing some components of a person's baseline economic life but not others, and redistributive taxation should employ whatever combination of tax bases is most efficient in promoting the relevant conception of equality of opportunity. On these views, the choice of tax base, at least for redistributive purposes, is purely pragmatic.

VIII.   Endowment and the Value of Autonomy

If distributive justice consisted in equality of opportunity, somehow defined, so that differences in how people choose to use the same opportunities raised no issue of justice, then it might seem to follow that tax burdens should not depend on people's choices either. Of two people with the same potential income but different actual incomes, the person with the lower actual income could not complain at paying the same tax as the other since they are equally situated, so far as economic justice is concerned. From this perspective, indeed, it is the income tax that is unfair, because it penalizes certain choices: the beachcomber enjoys leisure tax-free, whereas the MBA enjoys caviar and champagne only after contributing a significant proportion of its cost to the fisc. As we saw in chapter 2, there are also efficiency arguments that favor taxing endowment: as a lump-sum tax, a tax on potential earnings has no substitution effect and—choosing among lump-sum taxes—it seems likely to have better incentive effects than a head tax.[67] But in the end no one defends endowment taxation.

One problem always noted is that the government would not be able to collect the necessary information about people's earning potential. But there is also the moral objection that endowment taxation would effectively force work on those who could otherwise survive without wage earnings and likewise force many people who would prefer a lower-paying position into careers that they have no interest in.[68]

For equal opportunity theorists, who reject welfare as the appropriate metric for assessing distributive outcomes, the value of freedom of action thus compromised must be understood in deontological terms—perhaps as a right to do whatever one likes so long as it does not infringe the rights of others. If the rights of others recognized by the theory are a narrow set of negative rights, this is a hard view to square with many uncontroversial positive legal duties—such as the duty to file a tax return.[69]

Mill's consequentialist account of the value of freedom of action as a component of welfare faces no such problem. And it does not seem controversial to include this good, the good of being able to decide for oneself how to act from among a suitably broad range of options, in the metric for the assessment of social outcomes. On the other hand, this view leaves it less clear to what extent such freedom should be protected as a right, rather than merely as one good among others.

How great an interference with autonomy would it be to tax people an amount determined by the earnings they could have, whether they have those earnings or not? It is true that this would lead people to choose otherwise than they would in the absence of the tax, but, of course, taxation of actual earnings does that too. Robert Nozick famously argued that taxation of earnings was for this reason "on a par with forced labor";[70] to achieve their preferred level of explicit consumption, people are forced to work more than they would need to in a tax-free world. We may assume that this argument is not dispositive against taxation of earnings, but what distinguishes it from the argument against endowment taxation?

The difference can only be one of degree. In the first place, we should not accept Nozick's way of putting the point. There can be no principled objection to the mere fact that enforcement of the legal obligation to pay tax forcibly limits the alternatives available to us.[71] Enforcement of the criminal law, traffic laws, zoning laws, and many other legal duties has the same effect. Moreover, as we have observed, there is no reason to be protective of the hypothetical choices that would be available in the imaginary no-tax world.

Nevertheless, the value of autonomy should lead us to prefer a set of institutions that limits the range of choices as little as possible, by comparison with other feasible sets of *actual* institutions. And the extent to which endowment taxation restricts people's choices is extreme, compared to familiar forms of taxation of earnings. Thus, while no person can be a sculptor without some source of income, and taxation of earnings increases the amount of work (cleaning houses, perhaps) required, a trained corporate lawyer taxed according to $500,000 in potential annual earnings will find that the time for sculpture is reduced almost to zero. So we can say that endowment taxation can be a far greater hindrance to a chosen career than ordinary taxation of earnings. But what seems most objectionable about such a case is that the lawyer may be condemned by his training to only one feasible line of work—corporate lawyering. If this is right, the problem is not so much that endowment taxation forces people to do what they would prefer not to do, but that it may leave people with literally one option in life. This is an extreme interference with autonomy that should weigh heavily against any contribution to aggregate welfare an endowment tax would make.

The positive impact on levels of welfare from the implementation of an endowment tax seems in any case to be doubtful. The income effect of the tax would lead many more people to choose higher-paid careers than they otherwise would. Perhaps this is in itself good, since productivity would rise. But it would also keep more able people away from lower paid though socially valuable work. Most creative and performing artists—painters, novelists, poets, composers, violinists, pianists—could make more doing something else. The same is probably true of many academics and teachers. An endowment tax, if it were workable, would have the profound social effect of reducing the number of entrants to these labor-intensive and somewhat risky fields and probably raising their cost. It is not obvious, in other words, that the most good comes when the people who can earn the most always choose to earn the most. And under an endowment tax scheme, even more people than otherwise would be doing work that they don't like, with consequent bad effects on the quality of work, not to mention the welfare of the workers.[72]

These reasons for rejecting an endowment tax as part of the best institutional scheme may seem to be too weak. Wouldn't it be outrageous to contemplate taxing harmless Malibu surfers who survive on a small part-time income, thus forcing them to work full time and at maximum salary? To many, the impact of the endowment tax on the choice between working and not working for pay makes its interference with autonomy seem different in kind from that of a tax on earnings.

But it isn't really a difference in kind, only a difference in degree. Daniel Shaviro makes two telling points in this regard. First, there is the matter of imputed income. The Malibu surfer has no explicit consumption but plenty of implicit or imputed consumption. If there were some magical way of reducing the surfer's fun by a certain amount and transferring that benefit to the treasury, then the choice not to work would be no obstacle to taxation. To bring out the point from the other perspective, Shaviro asks us to imagine that Wall Street lawyers were paid in yogurt that spoiled within five minutes if not eaten, so that to pay their taxes they would have to go off to clean federal office buildings after hours. The point here is not that endowment taxation raises no autonomy concerns given the actual facts about how taxes can be collected, but rather that there is no intrinsic moral objection to taxing people who do not earn wages.[73]

Equally significant is Shaviro's second point. He notes that it is widely understood, with no great alarm, that a tax increase on the earnings of one family member may force another to choose some paid work over no paid work.[74] If this is not outrageous, why is the equivalent effect on the surfer?

The principal ethical objection to endowment taxation is not that it forces people to work, but that, compared to familiar consumption or income taxation, it would constitute a much more radical interference with autonomy. Given this, and given the dubiousness of the welfare gains an endowment tax would bring, it would not be a serious option, even if the information required for its implementation were available.

IX. Exclusions and Credits

Whether the tax base is consumption, income, or consumption plus wealth, there are a host of more specific questions about whether certain special kinds of consumption should *not* be taxed. As already noted, economists tell us that "cleaner" tax bases are less distortionary and thus cost us all less. This puts the burden of proof on those who favor any particular exclusion or deduction from the tax base. Similarly, convincing reasons, of administrative cost or otherwise, are required to justify the nontaxation of imputed consumption; here the most discussed case—one where taxation would not be hopelessly infeasible—is the imputed consumption enjoyed by people who own their own homes and who therefore live rent-free.[75] (For simplicity, we will from now on use the word "exclusions" to include deductions and the nontaxation of imputed consumption, since these are economically equivalent.)[76] Are there reasons of justice that count for or against any of the familiar array of exclusions?

As we explain more fully in chapter 8, concerns about the horizontal equity of, say, the tax treatment of housing are misplaced—for the by now familiar reason that justice does not require us to preserve pretax equalities in welfare or opportunities. The issues of justice raised by exclusions turn, as with the proper tax treatment of wealth, on the impact of the various special kinds of consumption on people's welfare or opportunities[77] and the implications of this for the tax system understood as a means to the achievement of just social outcomes.

To take a straightforward example, money spent on medical services does not make a person better off than someone without such expenses; further, health care expenses are not, generally, proportionate to overall consumption. So any attempt to bring about a more equal distribution of welfare by taxing those who consume more and transferring the money to those who consume less will miss its mark if health care expenses are fully included in the consumption base.

From an equal opportunity perspective, this issue is more complicated, with different theories treating medical bad luck differently—on some accounts this is a source of inequality that should be compensated for, on others it is not. It depends on what kinds of bad luck are thought to fall within the scope of social justice. The existence of voluntary insurance schemes would also affect the reasoning.[78]

The issue would be partly defused by an adequate system of universal health insurance. Though there would still be individuals who could and would spend more on medical treatment than was provided by the universal coverage, at a certain point the welfare lost through such expenditures may properly be regarded as falling outside the scope of collective responsibility. Favorable tax treatment of any expenditure constitutes a transfer to those who make that choice from those who do not. As we explain more fully in chapter 8, even though such transfers cannot be condemned on the spurious ground of horizontal inequity, they still have to be justified.

If one decides, however, that medical expenditures should have an effect on taxation, the question is whether a full or partial tax credit would be preferable to an exclusion. In a system with graduated rates, exclusions from the tax base provide a greater benefit to those in higher tax brackets who are eligible for them. This makes sense on traditional ability-to-pay grounds, since the medical expense is treated as if it was money you never had. But if we evaluate tax provisions by their effects on social outcomes, an exclusion is a poor choice, since rich people do not lose more welfare from spending a given sum on health care than do poor people; on the contrary. A tax credit, by contrast, reduces a person's taxes by the same amount regardless of the total tax bill. This is a more accurate adjustment in people's welfare, since for each person the tax break provides a benefit of the same size as the loss occasioned by spending that much money on health care rather than something else. (There is apparently a trend among OECD countries to replace exclusions with credits.[79])

Each existing exclusion under U.S. tax law raises its own complicated issues that have been much discussed; we will not attempt a survey here.[80] It is worth making some points about the so-called charitable deduction, however. The word charity suggests that this deduction is a means of decentralizing the process by which a community discharges its collective responsibility to alleviate the worst aspects of life at the bottom of the socioeconomic ladder. Since there is disagreement about what the exact nature of that responsibility is, and about which are the most efficient agencies, it is arguably a good idea for the state to subsidize individuals' contributions to agencies of their choice rather than itself making all the decisions about the use of public funds for this purpose. But even if that is so, the existing deduction cannot be defended on those grounds, because many currently deductible "charitable" contributions go to cultural and educational institutions that have nothing to do with the poor, the sick, or the handicapped.[81] State funding of such institutions may or may not be desirable, but the argument would be very different, and "charity" is hardly the right word.

In any event, a flat rate tax credit for contributions to qualifying nonprofit organizations would be preferable in our view to a deduction. If the aim is to allow private individuals to decide how such funds should be directed away from the treasury, the current system is defective for allowing those in higher tax brackets a greater say.

Progressivity means that more support in forgone taxes is given by all of us to the charitable choices of the rich than to those of the middle classes and the poor. This effect is magnified by the fact that most taxpayers of modest income don't itemize their charitable contributions, but take the standard deduction.

A significant argument on the other side of the issue is that higher total contributions might well be induced by a deduction than by a credit at the same total cost in tax revenue, if the response of the rich to the tax value of their contributions is highly elastic by comparison with that of the unrich. The question then would become: Does the fact that a deduction shakes more money loose, per tax dollar forgone, outweigh the fact that the extra money goes to causes favored by the rich?[82]

X. Transitions

We have argued that the income tax is not unfair to savers. More generally, we have argued that justice in taxation is a matter of securing certain outcomes, rather than a matter of impacting fairly on a certain baseline distribution of resources or welfare. In this sense, tax justice is about outcomes. But that does not mean that only outcomes are relevant to tax policy, because the path to a just outcome can also raise questions of justice. When changes are made to ongoing institutional arrangements, there is an important backward-looking concern, that of the protection of reasonable expectations. Given that any change for the better is, indeed, a change, this is a very important practical issue. To use Martin Feldstein's terminology, we never face issues of tax design, but rather always issues of tax reform.[83]

It is believed that a switch from an income tax to a consumption tax would impose a one-time tax on existing wealth—since wealth would become subject to tax when withdrawn for consumption, even though its accumulation had already been subject to income tax.[84] As with any such transitional effect, this greatly complicates the question of whether, from the point of view of distributive justice, such a switch would be for the better all things considered. The problem is not just figuring out what such a once-off tax would mean for absolute and relative levels of welfare, or opportunities; one must also factor in the effects of people's decisions made in anticipation of the change in scheme.[85]

But the importance of people's expectations is not just instrumental. Even if all significant tax changes could be kept fully secret till enacted, there would be the question of whether it is right to change the rules midway through people's lives. Even though no one may be entitled to any particular bundle of resources in the abstract sense, a plausible norm of political morality has it that we are entitled to enjoy what we had reason to believe would be the consequences of our choices under the prevailing institutional arrangement. The norm of protecting reasonable expectations may be explained by appeal to some notion of fair play, but it seems more importantly to be connected to the value of autonomy and the particular interest people have in being able to make reasonably settled plans for the future.[86]

How far expectations ought to be protected depends on how reasonable those expectations are. It is not reasonable to expect that government economic policy will remain fixed across decades, and there is plenty of scope for planning one's life against a background of changing policies on government debt reduction, the minimum wage, or environmental protection. But, for example, it would be contrary to reasonable expectations to suddenly abolish the home mortgage interest deduction without any relief for those with already existing mortgages. The one-time tax burden on existing wealth holders from the transition to a consumption tax would fall into the same category.

This does not mean that the transition is forbidden as a matter of justice. Rather, it calls for the adoption of transition rules the purpose of which would be to bring the one-time burden down within the scope of what might be reasonably expected; or at least to move somewhat in that direction.

On balance, however, we do not think there is a case from the point of view of justice for moving to a consumption tax base in the first place. If anything, we are sympathetic to a greater use of taxes to tap disparities in wealth, to the extent that this can be done, as well as disparities in consumption. An important aspect of such efforts is the taxation of intergenerational transfers, which we will address in chapter 7.

6

Progressivity

I. Graduation, Progression, Incidence, and Outcomes

Graduated rates are a political issue. Prior to July 1, 2001, the highest marginal rate in the U.S. personal income tax was 39.6%.[1] That figure alone suggests political concern about the number "40." In fact, the figure served to conceal the fact that a phase-out of itemized deductions and personal exemptions for high-income earners brings the effective marginal rate above 40% for some people.[2]

The political rhetoric offered on behalf of flat tax schemes of one sort or another also focuses heavily on the nominal rate structure. Here is a quote from the "Flat Tax" web site maintained by House Majority Leader Dick Armey and Senator Richard Shelby to promote their "Freedom and Fairness Restoration" bill, introduced into the U.S. Congress in 1999:[3]

> The flat tax will restore fairness to the tax law by treating everyone the same. No matter how much money you make, what kind of business you're in, whether or not you have a lobbyist in Washington, you will be taxed at the same rate as every other taxpayer.[4]

Even on its own terms, this statement is false, since the Armey/Shelby proposal provides for a sizable exemption for low-income earners, \$25,000 for a family of four, with the result that many people would pay no tax.[5]

But the important point is that marginal rate structures are three steps removed from any serious issue of distributive justice. First, what matters for the distribution of tax burdens is average rather than marginal rates of tax. Due to the exemption, the average rates under the Armey/Shelby flat tax are progressive throughout the income range; so in the only sense of "rate" that matters to the traditional understanding of tax fairness, taxpayers would not pay tax at the same rate under that scheme.[6]

Second, the person legally responsible for paying a tax does not necessarily bear its economic burden. Thus, for example, it is typically thought that employees bear the burden of payroll taxes payable by employers.[7] Economists have devoted considerable effort to the problems of tax incidence; incidence assumptions are obviously crucial in the preparation of the "distribution tables" that aim to inform legislators about the distributions of burdens different tax schemes would produce.[8]

In any event, and this the third step, information about the actual incidence of tax burdens is of instrumental importance only. What matter are the larger-scale results. A government aiming to improve the justice of social outcomes needs to know whether a given change in the tax law will increase or reduce inequality, the level of welfare of the worst off, equality of opportunity, and so on. The real issue of political morality is the extent to which social outcomes are just, and knowledge of the distribution of real tax burdens is important only insofar as it helps us advance that aim.*

This vitiates the classic discussion by Blum and Kalven, which proceeds almost entirely by evaluating progressivity

---

*The argument of fairness offered by President Bush in 2001 for cutting taxes across the board took yet a further step away from reality. His claim was that everybody should get a tax cut, and that it would be unfair to single out lower income earners, for example. This assumes not only that pretax market outcomes are just, but that the existing tax scheme takes the right proportion from everyone.

in terms of traditional tax equity standards alone, rather than in terms of larger standards of societal justice. There is one point late in the essay, however, where they poignantly concede the problem of narrowness in the traditional approach:

> One can only sympathize with Henry Simons in insisting that, in any discussion of progression, the problem of inequality "be dragged out into the open." Certainly both on grounds of candor and clarity this is commendable. It nevertheless has one overwhelming difficulty. In a study of progression, as soon as the issue of economic inequality has been dragged out into the open, we discover that we have lost our topic."[9]

What it shows, of course, is that they were discussing the wrong topic.

II. Assessment of Outcomes

In addition to their differences about rights, liberty, and procedural fairness, different theories of justice apply different criteria to social outcomes; these criteria require, in turn, different kinds of information.[10] Thus, if equality of welfare matters in itself, a choice must be made among different possible measures of inequality (such as the GINI coefficient). On the priority view, according to which a just state will promote the welfare of all people but give priority to the welfare of those worse off, or on Rawls's difference principle, all that matters is how well-off people are, not degrees of inequality as such. Such views thus do not require a decision about measures of inequality, even though Rawls's view, at least, is egalitarian in its inspiration.[11]

Of course, even if equality of welfare is held to be an end in itself, it could not plausibly be thought to be the only social good; rather, it must be weighed against the value of overall levels of welfare.[12] Like utilitarianism, then, all the egalitarian views just mentioned require information about welfare and count higher levels of welfare as improvements in the justice of a social outcome, all else being equal.

Welfare is a complex value; depending on the preferred metric, government must make use of information such as hours of leisure, health indicators, living conditions, literacy and education, along with consumption and wealth. The tax system is implicated in all these factors as the revenue source for public education, health care, etc.; but insofar as differential tax rates are themselves part of the means to a more just outcome, consumption and wealth are the relevant factors. The aim, for a welfare-based theory of justice, is to adjust levels of taxation and cash transfer so that prevailing levels of consumption and wealth are more just than they otherwise would be.

Not all aspects of welfare can be measured directly; proxies must be used. But equality of opportunity theories of justice face even more severe informational problems. If the proxies for welfare are well chosen, we can have confidence in getting the assessment of outcomes roughly right. When the criterion of justice asks not how well off people are but rather how well off they could be—what their opportunities are and have been in life—there seems to be no available proxy that will guide us, even roughly. (Asking people to reveal to the tax collector their potential earnings, so far as they know them, is unlikely to produce the truth.)

The more egalitarian the theory, the worse the problem. Thus, equal libertarianism holds a society just if differences in opportunity due to educational and social background *and* natural talent are compensated for. Since we have no meter for natural talent, it is impossible, even in a world of equal material resources at the start of life, to know whether a person's greater or lesser prosperity is due to natural factors or to choice.

Fair equality of opportunity is somewhat more measurable, since it requires only equality of start-of-life financial resources and education. But, of course, equal opportunity to develop given talents is not just a matter of equal funding for schools. As Rawls notes, "the extent to which natural capacities develop and reach fruition is affected by all kinds of social conditions and class attitudes. Even the willingness to make an effort, to try, and so to be deserving in the ordinary sense is itself dependent upon happy family and social circumstances."[13] If that is true it would be very hard to tell whether fair equality of opportunity has been achieved. Rawls himself asserts that its achievement is "impossible in practice."[14]

Having said all that, we may be able to circumvent some of these esoteric questions in the following way. For the purpose of assessing the progressivity of a tax scheme, the social values that will matter most are those having to do with equality and inequality. As we have seen, there is a wide range of views about the responsibility of a society for the economic welfare of its members, particularly the worst off. At one extreme is the libertarian position that the sole function of government is to protect people against violation of their negative rights—rights against force, fraud, theft, and violence—and that provision of positive goods, from subsistence on up, is a private matter. Then there are those who would add a government responsibility for the provision of certain public goods like environmental protection, education, postal service, and highways. But most people go further and accept some social duty on the part of the government to promote the material welfare of individuals and to provide them with some of the resources needed to pursue their own interests in life.

The responsibility may be defined in different ways and at different levels. Some may hold only that the state should ensure that there is a social safety net, to prevent anyone from falling into extreme want. Others may hold that there should be public policies that provide everyone with positive equality of opportunity to compete for social and economic success. Others may favor a more comprehensive concern for advancing the welfare of everyone. If they are utilitarians, they will favor policies that maximize the total benefit of everyone in the society. If they hold a priority view, or accept Rawls's difference principle, they will favor policies that particularly benefit those at the bottom of the social and economic ladder.

Disagreements about the extent of public responsibility are not going to disappear; they are the essence of politics. But we would make the following point: In spite of the disagreements, there is an important area of agreement among those views that take government responsibility for the welfare of citizens seriously. Whether one is a utilitarian or a Rawlsian or a priority theorist, or a believer in a social safety net, or a defender of fair equality of opportunity, or of equal libertarianism, one will be concerned about poverty.

Poverty is bad from all these points of view. The lives of the poor are hard, often humiliating; children born poor have fewer opportunities and lower expectations. However you slice it, an increase in the resources of poor people will do a lot of good, per dollar—more good than a comparable increase in the resources of those who have more, or much more. That is the most general and straightforward basis for redistributive policies, and it holds in some degree for a wide range of views this side of libertarianism.

From the point of view of mainstream theories of justice, therefore, the evaluation of the results of a tax scheme will, at a minimum, depend heavily on two things: first, whether it can raise enough revenue to provide for an adequate level of public goods like defense, law enforcement, and education; and second, whether it results in a decent standard of living for the least economically advantaged members of the society. It is clear that either a utilitarian or a more egalitarian standard will require us to care about this.

So to some extent we can take as representative, for the purpose of evaluating degrees of tax progressivity, the method of assessment in terms of effects on aggregate welfare, effects which will be importantly dependent on the welfare of those at the bottom of the social ladder. Any conception of justice that is concerned with the welfare and equal opportunities of the members of the society—whether or not it gives special weight to the worst off—will have to be particularly concerned with the standard of living of those who are poorest. We will therefore limit ourselves, in the rest of this chapter, to theories of distributive justice that assess outcomes in terms of welfare.

III. Optimal Taxation

There is a distinguished economics literature on optimal tax and transfer rates, dating back to an article by James Mirrlees in 1971.[15] This literature is extremely important for the study of justice in taxation. Most significantly, it approaches the topic in the right way, investigating outcomes rather than the distribution of burdens. The normative parameters of optimal tax analysis, which are those of welfare economics, are in our opinion too narrow to allow it to produce a full account of tax justice, but its results nevertheless provide information essential for the implementation of any nonlibertarian conception of justice.

Its central question is what level of taxation would best promote welfare (either weighted in favor of the worse off or not), given the welfare losses caused by the behavioral effects of an income tax. Any theory of justice concerned about levels of welfare, including a theory that gives intrinsic weight to greater equality (though such theories are not usually considered in the optimal tax literature), must confront the fact that while taxes enable redistribution from richer to poorer, they may also depress work effort and thus reduce overall welfare.

It is marginal tax rates that are relevant for the effect on labor: a person's decision whether to work an additional hour is determined by the tax payable on that extra hour, not the tax payable on the hours already worked. So if the effect of taxation on labor is a serious concern, marginal rates ought to be as low as possible. The lower the rates, however, the less revenue collected. Thus, optimal tax analysis sets out to determine, for different criteria of justice in outcomes, the right trade-off between revenue raised and welfare lost due to the effect on how hard and how much people choose to work.

In addition to graduated tax brackets, starting with zero, a more radical mechanism for redistribution is standardly assumed in optimal tax models: instead of a sizable tax-exempt bracket at the bottom, a positive demogrant that goes to everyone, where the demogrant is equivalent to an exemption of tax on all income up to a certain point, and to a negative income tax for those who fall below that point.* In many analyses, the optimal result, whether the criterion for the as-

---

*At a marginal rate of 50%, for example, a $15,000 demogrant would be equivalent to a complete exemption from tax of the first $30,000 earned, or a $5,000 tax rebate for someone who earned only $20,000.

sessment of outcomes weights the interests of the worse off or not, is surprising: a sizable demogrant combined with taxation at flat or declining marginal rates—including even rates that decline to zero at the top of the income distribution.[16]

Each different model of optimal taxation makes different assumptions and each set of assumptions is contestable.[17] But the most important assumption concerns the prevalence and size of the effect on labor supply—and all models assume its existence, to a greater or less extent. They assume that marginal taxes will make working and earning less attractive. The trouble is that the empirical evidence suggests that in respect of the choice between labor and leisure this effect is, in fact, rather rare, at least for the kinds of marginal rates that have actually been in effect. (An important exception to this is the behavior of potential second earners in a marriage—an equity question we will take up in chapter 8.) Slemrod and Bajika write that "nearly all research concludes that male participation and hours worked respond hardly at all to changes in after-tax wages and therefore to marginal tax rates."[18]

This would significantly weaken the importance of the optimal tax literature as a guide to policy. In recent years, however, particularly since an article by Martin Feldstein in 1995, economists have turned their focus from the effect of taxes on labor supply to their effect on taxable income. There are many ways a person can alter taxable income other than by varying labor supply; examples include changes in levels of savings and the content of portfolios, the timing of income, nontaxable forms of compensation, levels of avoidance and evasion, and levels of deductions.[19] Any such response to taxes may cause a loss in overall welfare. Feldstein estimated that the effect of taxation on taxable income was very pronounced, especially for higher income earners; subsequent work has produced less dramatic, though still significant estimates of the size of this behavioral response.[20] In a recent optimal tax analysis based on the responsiveness of taxable income to marginal rates, the result for a criterion of justice that gives priority to the welfare of the worse off was a significant demogrant ($11,000), coupled with high but declining marginal rates.[21]

This is very much work in progress and it could not be said that a professional consensus has been reached on the responsiveness of taxable income to marginal rates. An ongoing problem is controlling for changes in taxable income unrelated to the tax reforms of the 1980s and 1990s that are the focus of this research.[22] We do not try to take a stand in this debate. Nevertheless, the focus on the effect of taxation on taxable income rather than labor supply can be misleading. While government can do little to change people's preferences over work and leisure, it can, through the structure of the tax system and otherwise, alter the ability of people to change their taxable income by means other than working less. As Slemrod has pointed out, the extent to which these nonlabor factors respond to tax rates is itself in good part a matter of government policy.[23]

It remains unclear, therefore, that declining marginal rates would be needed to generate the revenue that would finance a substantial demogrant. There is an important moral to the tale nevertheless: Results and not tax rates are what matter.

In the first place, the clash between the central role of the demogrant in optimal tax theory and contemporary public opinion about economic justice is extreme: few people believe in a guaranteed minimum income.[24] But once we loosen the grip of everyday libertarianism, there is no reason to rule out in advance what is, after all, one possible means among others for achieving our collective social goals. The same can be said about the fate of graduated rates. Whether or not optimal tax theorists will converge on the superiority of declining marginal rates (for plausible criteria of justice in outcomes), the exercise makes dramatically clear that the justice of a tax scheme cannot be intuited from a glance at the distribution table—let alone the rate table. We have to get used to looking past the surface of the tax law to the social outcomes it affects.

But there is one very important point to make about economists' lessons on the distinction between ends and means. If we are told that lower marginal rates coupled with a demogrant would be better even from the point of view of a strongly egalitarian theory of justice than graduated rates with a high marginal rate at the top, that gives us absolutely no reason to abandon high marginal rates *without* introducing a demogrant. This is blindingly obvious. But in practice the point is frequently ignored. It is frequently claimed, for example by Joseph Stiglitz, that the conclusions of optimal tax theory were an influence on the trend to much lower marginal rates in the 1980s.[25] This trend has been linked not with a greater role for cash transfers, but rather the reverse.[26] No one concerned with welfare, not even utilitarians, can regard the growing inequality that has characterized the last two decades in the United States[27] as an improvement from the point of view of justice. It is possible that, in its short-run practical consequences, economists' interest in the behavioral effects of taxation has done more harm than good to the cause of social justice.

IV. Tax Reform

Tax reformers need to be guided by considered judgments about the appropriate aims of government in a just society. To translate those aims into economic policy, government needs information about the levels of welfare (as measured by the appropriate metric) enjoyed by different groups in society along with, perhaps, a measure of inequality. It also needs information about the effects of various changes in tax and transfer policy on economic behavior; here it must rely on economists' empirical research and perhaps also trial and error.

Distribution tables remain important, but only to the extent that they permit us to compare the after-tax results of different policies. For example, if justice gives priority to improvement in the living standard of the worst-off group, a distribution table showing the change in disposable income for each income class will show whether the reform is for the better, other effects being equal. Finally, the degree of progressivity in the tax scheme will also be affected by the government's attempt to provide an appropriate level of public goods; as we have seen in chapter 4, this ideally turns on information about the marginal utilities of public and private expenditures for people with different levels of income and wealth.

The standard of justice for evaluating social outcomes is a disputed question of political morality. The best means to achieve any given set of aims is a disputed question of practical economics. Intense disagreement about both questions will surely always be with us, so the question, "How progressive should the rate structure be?" is not easy to answer. But the difficulty of the question should not be confused with emptiness or indeterminacy.

Henry Simons said that the criterion of ability to pay could justify any level of regression or progression that you liked.[28] He was right because that criterion *is* empty; disagreements about what is a fair share of the tax burden turn on no genuine issue of moral principle; they are disagreements about nothing. But disagreements about social justice are not about nothing. It would be foolish to expect unanimity or finality about the range of moral issues canvassed in chapters 3 and 4, or about the economic issues that determine the choice of institutional means. But it would be equally foolish to think that there are not better or worse answers to these questions.

Our own sympathies lie with those conceptions of justice that require a society to aim at providing at least a decent minimum level of welfare and access to opportunity for everyone. This view suggests careful consideration of two kinds of progressivity in the tax system. First, the progressivity of a substantial demogrant, resulting in a negative income tax (cash transfers) to the lowest earners. Second, the progressivity of marginal rates, where the distribution of income is very unequal. The latter is empirically the more difficult question, since it depends on incentive effects and the possibilities of income shifting for tax avoidance. But the available evidence does not seem to establish that a flat or declining marginal rate is necessary to generate the revenues needed to provide adequately for those at the bottom.

The provision of a basic social minimum satisfies a humanitarian or mildly egalitarian conception of justice. But a serious moral case can be made for more strongly egalitarian views. We are persuaded that a society's institutions should promote the welfare of the worst off well beyond what most people would count as the required minimum—at the expense, if necessary, not only of the welfare of the best off but also of total welfare, the total size of the pie. This is not the view that equality matters above all, so that even equal misery is better than inequality; nobody advocates such a conception of justice. The ideal is rather that of a community committed to making the lives of all its members better; what makes the view egalitarian is the conviction that so long as there is poverty, exceptional weight should be given to the interests of those who are worst off.

It is a clear implication of such a view that a move in the direction of justice could entail significant loss in disposable income and wealth for those who are now best off—not because that would be good in itself, but because those resources are, morally speaking, better used elsewhere, and it is legitimate for the legal system to rearrange property rights to this end if it can do so effectively. If we embrace such a conception, we will conclude that the tax and transfer system of a just capitalist society will have among its functions the redistribution of gross earnings and wealth. Depending on economic effects, the best mechanism may well involve, in addition to a sizable demogrant, substantially progressive marginal rates.

Currently, the United States does not provide a basic social minimum and thus falls short of even the more laissez-faire of the two conceptions of justice we have mentioned. Given this fact, the current tax reform climate is morally perverse, on any plausible view: massive tax cuts for the rich, the abolition of the estate tax, the abolition of graduated rates—these are all steps in the direction of greater injustice, and the first two steps have now been taken.[29] In real politics the issue is unfortunately not only moral and empirical but also rhetorical or ideological. "It's your money, not the government's!" remains a potent appeal against the claim that a significant portion of the social product would do more good if made available to low earners than if left in the hands of the top earners and their heirs. We say more about this aspect of the problem in the final chapter.

7

Inheritance

I. The "Death Tax"

In 1997, the highest-earning 1% of the population of the United States accounted for around 17% of all income earned. But the distribution of wealth was skewed even more to the top end. Figures for 1998 show the wealthiest 1% of households holding around 38% of total wealth, and the wealthiest 20% holding around 83% of the total.[1] As noted in chapter 5, estimates of the proportion of all wealth that is inherited vary greatly, but the rough average of the various estimates is 50%.[2] Evidently, the inheritance of wealth is a major source of economic inequality in this class-unconscious society.

Because of high exemptions and the possibility of avoidance, estate and gift taxes have never made a significant impact on inherited fortunes; they typically yield about 1% of total federal revenues.[3] Political support for such taxation has never been strong, and remarkably enough it has only got weaker in the face of increasing inequality in the distribution of wealth.[4] This trend came to a head in June 2001, when President George W. Bush signed the Economic Growth and Tax Relief Reconciliation Act, which gradually reduces estate and gift taxes starting in 2002 and repeals the estate tax altogether in 2010. Because of the Act's expiration at the end of 2010, however, the estate tax is now set to disappear for only one year.[5] Obviously, there will have to be further tax legislation before 2011; whether the estate tax will, in fact, be abolished from 2010 remains to be seen.

During his election campaign Mr. Bush frequently emphasized his opposition to the "death tax." In the final presidential debate, when asked why he favored the total abolition of the estate tax rather than restricting its impact, Mr. Bush replied, in part:

> I just don't think it's fair to tax people's assets twice regardless of your status. It's a fairness issue. It's an issue of principle, not politics.[6]

The estate tax has long been a charged political issue—in which the plight of family farmers and small business owners looms large; but many now seem to agree with President Bush that the taxation of gratuitous transfers of wealth raises a distinct issue of principle.[7]

That issue cannot be the number of times an asset is taxed, however. It is hard to be sure whether the objection is mere demagoguery or actual confusion. Taxes are not like punishments, which may not be imposed twice for the same crime. Nor is an inheritance tax like a second imposition of the very same income or sales tax on the same earnings or transaction. Multiple distinct taxes often tax people's assets "twice," as when a sales tax is imposed on the expenditure of someone's after-tax income, or a property tax is collected on an asset that was bought with income subject to tax. Any issue of fairness in such cases would have to be about the cumulative effect of multiple taxes, not about double taxation per se.

Looking at the issue in the traditional terms of the distribution of tax burdens, then, what matters is the total burden a person (not an asset) faces, compared with others.[8] Thus, "double taxation" of savings under the income tax is traditionally thought to be a problem (erroneously, as we argue in chapter 5) because it taxes savers more heavily than similarly situated current spenders. Not all bequests and gifts are taxed, so here the relevant comparison is between those who pay the combined estate and gift tax and those who do not. Under rules in effect in 2001, those who do pay are roughly the richest 2% of decedents.[9] A married couple can generally transfer $1.35 million in gifts and bequests before being liable for the tax; under the 2001 legislation, this amount increases to $2 million in 2002, with further increases to follow for the estate tax before its repeal. In addition, a couple may give up to $20,000 per year per recipient to other individuals free of tax; only amounts above that are counted against the maximum that may be transferred tax-free.[10] Leaving aside the substantial possibilities of avoidance,[11] people who do not pay the tax either have less income and wealth than those who do, or else they consume more.

Is it unfair to impose a greater tax burden on those with greater income and wealth? That, in traditional terms, is a vertical equity question, and such questions can be treated only in the larger context of distributive justice. Some commentators defend the gift and estate tax on the ground that it improves on an insufficiently progressive income tax.[12] There may even be sound efficiency reasons for this roundabout way of achieving a given level of progressivity if, for example, a tax on bequests is less distortionary than an income tax that raises the same revenue.[13] But the issue here is the entirely general one of progressivity; it has nothing whatever to do with "double taxation."

Could a distinct issue of fairness be raised about the estate tax under the traditional heading of horizontal equity? If two people have the same income during life—including gifts and bequests received—but have different amounts of wealth available for gratuitous transfers to others just because of different levels of consumption, it might be thought that fairness requires that they be taxed the same, not that the bigger donor be taxed more. Like the fairness-to-savers argument considered in chapter 5, this is just an application of the idea that the tax system should be "neutral" among alternative uses of resources or opportunities. We will not rehearse our rejection of that idea here.[14]

Putting the spurious problems of double taxation and horizontal equity aside, there are two genuine questions of principle in this area. First, should wealth that a person acquires by way of gratuitous transfer receive different tax treatment from wealth that is accumulated through earnings? Second, should wealth that is gratuitously transferred to another receive different tax treatment from wealth that is consumed in the form of goods and services? In other words, both from the perspective of the donee and from that of the donor, there is the question whether gratuitous transfers require special tax treatment.

We focus entirely on noncharitable gratuitous transfers. The question of the appropriate tax treatment of charitable gifts and bequests is discussed in chapters 5 and 8.

II. The Tax Base of the Donee

Under the current income tax, wealth accumulated by donors through saved earnings is taxed as it accumulates (ignoring for now the realization requirement), and no deduction is allowed for noncharitable gratuitous transfers. On the donee side, gifts and bequests are excluded from the income tax base; for bequests, there is a tax free step-up in basis, for the calculation of subsequent capital gains, to the value of the transferred asset at death.[15]

Is there any reason of justice to exclude gifts and bequests from the income (or consumption-plus-wealth) tax base of the donee? With the exception of transfers that fall into the category of support for children, the answer seems to be obviously no. Consumption and wealth figure in the tax base because of their relation to welfare, and it is clear that consumption and wealth from gratuitous receipts contribute at least as much to a person's welfare as do consumption and wealth made possible by earnings. This has been consistently recognized by defenders of broad-based income and consumption taxes over the years.[16] Exclusion of gifts and bequests from the donee's tax base is therefore on the face of it unwarranted and ought to require special justification.

As Bradford notes, however, while tax theorists typically regard exclusion of gratuitous receipts from the donee's tax base as odd, and while inheritance and accessions taxes are common elsewhere,[17] most Americans who are not tax theorists would probably regard inclusion as odd, indeed revolutionary.[18] Perhaps this is another case where the legal status quo has come to be regarded as naturally right, so that any departure from it by a change in the law seems wrong. No doubt an everyday libertarianism is also at work: If donors have full rights in their property, then they have the right to substitute the consumption of another for their own—without cost.

But there is another possible source for the intuitive sense that gratuitous receipts should not be taxed. It may be thought that such transfers take place in a private realm, where the government has no place. Even if the gifts are not among family members, they are not made to just anybody. Earnings, by contrast, are acquired in the public sphere, where transactions are made at arm's length and the regulative role of government is taken for granted.

Now there certainly is a legitimate concern for privacy associated with the taxation of gifts and bequests; at least, there is a concern about excessive bureaucratic intrusion. Everyone agrees on the need for an annual exemption for personal gifts up to some modest total value; this is in the interest of all, not only the rich. And the crucial, indeed legally mandated, role of the family in the bringing up of children requires that any transfers that count as bona fide child support should not be taxed to the recipient. Similar considerations justify the exemption from tax of transfers between spouses, and probably the exemption of bequests to a surviving spouse. (We return to these points in section IV.)

But these concerns clearly do not justify total immunity from taxation for gratuitous receipts. The sense that the government "has no business" in our personal, nonmarket transactions is based on a mistake. Good government makes a flourishing personal life possible just as much as it does civil society. But there comes a point where private transactions in their cumulative effects make a difference that is publicly important, and society must take notice. At that point, the personal becomes political and leaves the private sphere that is rightly protected against government intrusion. Most interpersonal gifts do not generate large economic consequences, but the intergenerational transmission of real wealth does;

it cannot claim the protection of privacy against taxation to the recipient.

In any event, taxes are not just fees charged for facilitating market-place transactions but are the means of raising revenue for public provision and the advancement of economic justice. Looked at in this light, the idea that a large gratuitous receipt should not be taxed seems absurd: It would mean that the person who works, gives up leisure, and contributes to economic life must share in society's collective burdens, while the person who gains a windfall without doing anything need not.

The only justification for not including (nonsupport, nontrivial) gratuitous receipts in the donee's income tax base would be administrative. Here a possible justification for the current approach under the income tax can be constructed. If we accepted the principle that, ideally, donees should be taxed and donors should receive a deduction for assets given away, we might see the absence of such a deduction as nevertheless a better way, administratively speaking, of taxing receipts to the donee. (For example, allowing a deduction for donors might encourage income shifting from higher- to lower-bracket family members.)[19] The plausible incidence assumption here is that the burden of the income tax on donors' transferred wealth is typically borne by donees, since donors end up transferring less than they would if they received a deduction.

There are two problems with this suggestion. First, there is no good reason to think that donors should ideally receive a deduction for gratuitous transfers, even if donees are liable for tax; we discuss this in the next section. Leaving that aside, there is a further objection. Even if the tax paid by the donor on assets gratuitously transferred is borne by the donee, it is levied at rates set by the economic circumstances of the donor, not those of the donee. But the point of including gratuitous receipts in the tax base of the donee is that these receipts contribute to the donee's welfare and so should be taken into account in the assessment of distributive outcomes. We cannot know what difference gratuitous transfers make to the appropriate tax burden for donees if we know nothing of the recipient's economic circumstances apart from the transfer. If the transfer is from a very rich person to a very poor person, who remains fairly badly off after the transfer, tax paid by the donor and borne by the donee may well worsen rather than improve the justice of economic outcomes. And outcomes are what we should be interested in.

For the same reason, adding a gift and estate tax to the current income tax does not fill the gap left by the exclusion of gratuitous receipts from the donee's taxable income. Even leaving aside the excessive current exemption levels and problems of avoidance, and even assuming that the burden of the transfer tax falls primarily on donees, the problem, once again, is that the tax is not sensitive to the economic circumstances of donees. As we will discuss in section V, there may be a case for taxing gratuitous transfers more heavily than other receipts and so a case for a separate wealth transfer tax over and above a properly inclusive income tax. But even if that is so, it would still be essential to fix the tax burden with reference to the donee's and not the donor's circumstances; any separate transfer tax should take the form of an inheritance or accessions tax. None of this is to deny that, if the income tax *does* exclude gifts and bequests from the donee's tax base, a gift and estate tax on the donor is better than nothing, from the point of view of justice.

Including gratuitous transfers in the tax base of donees would be a radical departure from current federal practice. On the other hand, the exclusion of gratuitous receipts is one of the most obvious and egregious failures of the current tax regime to take into account relevant information about people's economic circumstances. What possible rationale could there be for ignoring, for the purposes of distributive justice, the contribution to people's welfare that is made by inherited fortunes? We consider some efficiency-based reasons in section IV, but the important point is that, in the absence of strong reasons to the contrary, justice requires the taxation of (nontrivial, nonsupport) gratuitous receipts.

III. No Deduction for Donors

While tax theorists typically agree about the inclusion of receipts in the donee's tax base, there is some disagreement about whether, if that is done, donors should be allowed a deduction. The disagreement is best understood by considering first the appropriate treatment under a (cash-flow) consumption tax. Here the question is whether gifts and bequests count as consumption on the part of the donor, for if they are not, they should be deductible under a consumption tax. This cannot be answered simply by reflecting on the concept of consumption; rather, the issue is what contribution gifts and bequests make to the welfare of the donor. Not surprisingly, opinions differ. While it is clear that donors gain something from making the transfers, it is also clear that there is a difference between giving away a million dollars and buying goods and services with it. Not that the former always contributes less to welfare than the latter; at very high levels of consumption of goods and services, the reverse may be true.

But it seems to us that the discussion of whether to count gratuitous transfers as consumption is too narrowly focused—for the same reason that we reject sole reliance on a consumption base. The possession of wealth that can be given to one's family and others obviously contributes to welfare in a sense relevant to distributive justice. But especially in the case of the large bequests that are most important to distributive justice, it is superficial to analyze this contribution as the purchase of gratification through empathetic identification with the welfare of another, or a "warm glow" that accompanies the signing of the will (to mention two possibilities discussed in the economics literature.)[20] Rather, the satisfaction attending the ability to make sizable gifts and bequests is just one aspect of the composite contribution the possession of wealth makes to a person's welfare. The power to make gifts and bequests can be valuable even to people who don't exercise it—who die intestate with only the most vague testamentary plans (or knowledge of the law of intestate succession), or who die trying to make up their minds whether Andrew Carnegie was right that the almighty dollar would ruin their children.[21]

So it isn't necessary to decide why people make large gifts and bequests and how exactly it contributes to their happiness. What is undeniable is that wealth itself contributes to welfare and that for many people knowledge that this wealth can be passed on is one reason why it does. Voluntarily substituting another's consumption for one's own does not destroy this value. Whether the wealth is kept or given away, the wealthy person enjoys its benefits. The case against a deduction for donors does not depend on any theory about the pleasures of giving. When the contribution of wealth itself to a person's welfare is taken seriously, the case for the deduction simply vanishes.

This answers the question of whether gifts and bequests should be deductible by the donor under either a consumption tax or an income (or consumption-plus-wealth) tax. It might be objected that the argument we have made begs the question against a consumption base, which rejects the taxation of wealth as such. We would reply that reflection on whether gifts and bequests should count as consumption helps to bring out the inadequacy of a pure consumption base, reinforcing the arguments in chapter 5.

IV. Details and Objections

We have argued that gifts and bequests should be included in the income tax base of donees and that they should occasion no tax deduction for donors. So far, then, we conclude that gifts and bequests should receive favorable tax treatment neither from the perspective of the donor nor from that of the donee. In the next section we consider the possibility that gifts and bequests should be subject to more *stringent* tax treatment than wealth used for other purposes or acquired in other ways. But first we must add some details and consider some objections to what has been argued thus far.

Clearly, it is necessary to decide what should count as child support and what annual exemption should be allowed for small personal gifts without the intrusion of the IRS. Salient exemptions from the donee's tax base would include: an unlimited exemption for gifts between spouses, though not necessarily for bequests; an unlimited exemption for medical and educational services bought for dependent children; further exemptions for goods bought for dependent children that decline in value over time; a small annual exemption (say

$1,000 per donor-donee pair?) for personal gifts made to anyone.

This is not the place to attempt a detailed account; that has been done elsewhere.[22] The important thing is to state the principles that should determine the exemptions. They are, first, that taxation of support transfers—which would be borne largely by parents, since they would be reluctant to provide less support because of the tax—would amount to a burden on bringing up children as opposed to using resources in other ways. In a culture and legal system that imposes primary responsibility for the care of children on parents, this seems clearly inappropriate, as well as inconsistent with the provision of tax exemptions for dependents. The same principle would probably warrant exemption of support for other legal dependents—aged parents, for example. Second, intrusion into personal affairs by tampering with the distributional effects of small personal gifts would obviously do more harm than good from the point of view of economic justice. Whatever rules properly flow from these principles, it seems clear that they would not justify a tax-free transfer of $2 million from a couple to a child.

If a million dollar gift or bequest is included in the tax base of a donee in year one, but no further transfers are made for the next forty years, there is a "bunching" effect that could lead to an inaccurate assessment of the donee's economic position and therefore unwarranted taxation at higher marginal rates. Generally speaking, the relevant time perspective for distributive justice is not one year but a person's whole life; a year is simply an administratively tractable time period that seems to produce fairly accurate results from the whole-life perspective.[23] Accordingly, defenders of the inclusion of gifts and bequests in donees' income recommend an averaging device so that a bequest can be treated as if it had been made in installments over a longer period.[24]

In the political debate about "death" taxes, much concern is expressed for the plight of heirs who, because of the estate tax bill, are unable to carry on with a family business or farm. The threat has been grossly exaggerated for political reasons: The family farm is a much more sympathetic alleged victim of the estate tax than the family stock portfolio. But for whatever it is worth, the point applies equally to the taxation of bequests as income for the donee. The problem is one of liquidity and it is common to all forms of wealth taxation, including familiar property taxes. In the case of substantial bequests, however, the problem can be exacerbated by a bunching effect. There is a case for a reasonable exemption here, which together with averaging and perhaps also tax deferral devices like those already available under the estate tax can effectively minimize the threat to family-run enterprises.[25]

We will also comment on a few relatively technical questions commonly discussed by tax theorists. Would the inclusion of gratuitous receipts in donees' income discourage work or savings by potential donors?[26] It might, if a given donor would work harder or longer or consume less in order to make an untaxed gift but feels that the smaller-taxed gift that could be paid for by an hour of work or unit of forgone consumption does not justify the cost. Then again, work or savings might be encouraged, if a donor is set on transferring a gift of a certain net value. Taxation of gratuitous receipts might also encourage work or saving on the part of *donees*.[27] As always, there are both substitution and income effects in play, and empirical research is required to determine which is more important.[28] The consensus seems to be that a tax burden on gifts and bequests has little or no proven impact on donors' decisions whether to work or save.[29] In any event, the fact that a given tax reduces savings is hardly a dispositive objection to it, especially if there are other ways the government can promote capital investment and other reasons, such as distributive justice, to favor the tax.[30]

Louis Kaplow has argued that both transfer taxation and inclusion of gratuitous transfers in the tax base of donees discourage gift-giving, with resulting welfare losses.[31] On his analysis, gift-giving should be subsidized, not penalized. The argument goes like this. People give when they would gain from doing so. People gain from giving when the loss of utility the gift causes by reducing their wealth is outweighed by the utility derived from altruistic identification with the donee's interests and/or a "warm glow." That is, when deciding whether to give, people consider only their own good, not the good of the donees for their own sake. From the point of view of the social good, however, both count. Thus, a subsidy to the donor will promote the social good whenever, speaking roughly, it is both sufficient to move a donor to give rather than not and costs less in social terms than the total gain resulting from the gift.

Since most gifts and bequests of a size sufficient for inclusion in the donee's income are made by a well-off minority, the bad distributive effect of such a subsidy would surely outweigh, morally speaking, its contribution to aggregate welfare through its immediate effects on the donor and the recipient.[32] "On the merits," Joseph Dodge comments, "many would think that the government has better things to do than to improve welfare among the upper classes."[33] But Kaplow's argument suffers from a further problem. The claim that current levels of gift-giving are suboptimal depends upon an extremely reductive assumption about people's motivations, namely, that we always do only what we believe will be best for ourselves. Though this assumption, standard in welfare economics, may be near enough to the truth for the analysis of some aspects of market behavior, it is quite absurd in the context of gifts and bequests.[34] Just as it would be foolish to deny that donors are typically made better off by their ability to benefit donees, it is equally foolish to claim that donors are motivated solely by benefit to themselves. That leaves no place for what everyone knows to be extremely important motives such as a sense of family duty or of social role ("this is what people like us do").

But even if current levels of gift-giving are not suboptimal from the point of view of aggregate welfare, it might be thought that there is another reason not to impose an additional tax burden on gifts. People rich enough to make significant gifts will sometimes be choosing between a gift and their own consumption. Perhaps a tax on the gift at the donee's end will not deter the gift, even if that tax is borne by the donor. But just as some believe it wrong to tax supposedly more deserving savers more heavily than less-deserving spenders, even apart from incentive effects,* some

---

*This is the "common pool" argument discussed in chapter 5, section V.

might think it perverse to impose a penalty on the socially more beneficial choice to give rather than to consume.

If a couple gives a BMW to their child who has just left home, and the child must pay tax on the gift, this is a case where the tax is very likely to be borne—paid—by the donors. The result is that it costs the parents more to give their child a car than it costs to buy one for themselves.[35] Even assuming that the tax does not deter the gift, and even granting that the idea of double taxation can do no normative work, isn't it nevertheless regrettable to tax donors more than consumers?

This is a very specific kind of case: the donor must either want to shoulder the burden of the tax on the gift or else have no alternative; and the gift must be sufficiently valuable to trigger the tax. But the objection is in any case based on the implausible idea that taxes should track desert, or else the equally implausible idea that taxes should be neutral among consumption choices—the same ideas that underlie the analogous complaint about the treatment of savers under the income tax. Again, we will not repeat the reasons offered in chapter 5 against those arguments. It is true that, to the extent that a donor simply absorbs a donee's tax liability, the inclusion of the gift in the donee's tax base does not achieve its aim, which is to take account of the impact of the gift on the donee's economic position. Nor does it seem to serve any other good purpose. But it is impossible to prevent a donor from shielding a donee from tax burdens in this way.[36] Indeed, a striking feature of taxes on gratuitous transfers, whether legally levied on donors or on donees, is that their incidence can be determined by the donor. We can conclude that this type of case is an unavoidable side-effect of the proper tax treatment of gratuitous receipts—a side-effect which, while not in itself something to aim at, is also not objectionable from the point of view of justice, fairness, or efficiency.

V. Equal Opportunity and Transfer Taxation

We argued in chapter 5 that wealth contributes to welfare on any reasonable metric used for the assessment of economic justice and so should not be exempt from taxation—by way of an income tax or an annual wealth tax. If we assume that appropriate taxation of wealth or its accrual is in place, and suppose further that gratuitous receipts are included in the tax base of donees, is there any case for an additional tax on gratuitously transferred wealth? The Meade Committee Report states that

> inherited wealth is widely considered—and we share the view—to be a proper subject for heavier taxation [than wealth accumulated out of the owner's own earnings and savings] on grounds both of fairness and of economic incentives. The citizen who by his own effort and enterprise has built up a fortune is considered to deserve better tax treatment than the citizen who, merely as a result of the fortune of birth, owns an equal property; and to tax the former more lightly than the latter will put a smaller obstacle in the way of effort and enterprise.[37]

The fairness strand of this passage invokes equality of opportunity. The version of that ideal which would most strongly support an attack on inherited inequalities of wealth is the view that we have called equal libertarianism, so we will begin our discussion there, even though it is an outlying position from the point of view of the current political climate.

Equal libertarianism implies that, in the absence of practical obstacles or other reasons to the contrary (a very large qualification), gratuitous receipts should be confiscated by the state and redistributed equally among all persons.[38] That would be the only way to create a truly level playing field. If justice requires that each person have an equal opportunity to flourish in a given economic system, it must be prima facie unjust for some but not others to receive wealth and additional economic opportunities independently of their economic choices.

Even apart from practical considerations, those who accept this conclusion may believe that it is softened by further considerations of political morality, such as a concern that the personal donor-donee relationship not be in effect prohibited by the tax code, or a belief that people have the right to benefit others as they choose, rather than only through the impartial mechanism of the economic institutions of the state. When balanced against each other, the conflicting considerations will tend to the conclusion that, apart from the exemptions already mentioned for support and small gifts, gratuitous receipts should be taxed more heavily than wealth accumulated through earnings. So long as the tax is not completely confiscatory, gifts could still be made, and a limited right to benefit others according to choice would be respected.[39]

Suppose that these rather abstract moral considerations together yield some concrete conclusion about the extent to which gratuitously received wealth should be redistributed to advance the equal libertarian form of justice. The proper mechanism would be an accessions tax, where donees are taxed progressively on their cumulative receipts.[40] A tax levied on donors is ill suited to this conception of justice, since it is insensitive to the relative positions of potential donees— the people among whom (a degree of) equality of opportunity is required. And since the aim would be equality of opportunity across different lives, not persons per year, the tax should be calculated on a cumulative basis, with the amount of tax due on a particular receipt determined by a person's total gratuitous receipts to date. Lastly, progression would be required, since the greater the cumulative accession the greater the inequality of opportunity that is generated.

The Meade Committee Report notes a further complication. An ordinary accessions tax taxes the gifts and bequests when they are received; it is insensitive to how long the wealth is held by the donee.[41] This presumably matters, on an equality of opportunity theory, since once the wealth is given to someone else, the additional opportunity has gone. Thus, the Meade Committee recommended a Progressive Annual Wealth and Accessions Tax (PAWAT) that is designed precisely to tax gratuitously received wealth less if it is passed to someone else after a short time.

There are problems with the PAWAT.[42] Especially odd is that wealth consumed upon receipt is taxed the same as wealth held for the rest of a person's life; only gratuitous transfers to others are relevant for determining how long the wealth is held. One might reply that a person who consumed a bequest at 21 had the same opportunity as someone who held it until age 85, and so should be taxed the same. But this could also be said about a person who gave the wealth away at 21, since the opportunity to keep it existed. There seems to be no justification for the hybrid approach of the PAWAT.

We will not pursue the details of an optimal accessions tax. In our view, the fundamental reason of justice we have so far considered for such a tax—as an addition to a tax scheme that independently provides for adequate annual taxation of wealth and includes gratuitous receipts in the donee's tax base—is actually rather weak.[43] In previous chapters we have explained why we think that distributive justice cannot be understood solely in terms of equality of opportunity. The equal libertarian view gives too much weight to responsibility and choice in the evaluation of outcomes, and not enough to the outcomes themselves.

It is a different matter to embrace a principle of equality of opportunity as a supplement to principles of justice that apply to outcomes. Rawls, for example, though he regards the principle of fair equality of opportunity as inadequate on its own, ranks it prior in application to the difference principle, which applies to outcomes. On such an approach, outcomes are evaluated for justice independently of choice, but the availability of equal opportunity is regarded as a distinct and fundamental social value. What matters is that within a particular economic system people all have a reasonable chance to flourish—not that the economic system ensures that they will be responsible for where they end up, given the choices they make through life.[44]

This way of understanding the importance of choice and responsibility to distributive justice does not lead to the conclusion that there is a prima facie reason for confiscating gratuitous receipts. That is because it does not require strict *equality* of opportunity at all. A system where everyone of normal abilities has at least a reasonable opportunity to flourish under their own steam gives sufficient weight to choice and responsibility. Distributive justice in outcomes can take care of the rest.

Once we abandon the attempt to explain the whole of justice in terms of responsibility and choice under appropriate conditions, and instead add principles that require a just distribution of outcomes, the requirement of strict equality of opportunity seems unmotivated. (It is in any case unsatisfiable.) What matters in the domain of responsibility is that people have the ability to make their own way through life and that what happens to them is to a sufficient extent determined by their choices—not that they have the same opportunities to succeed in a particular economic system as everyone else.

Inequalities of economic opportunity above a decent minimum are not like the inequalities imposed by exclusionary discrimination on the grounds of sex, race, religion, or sexual orientation. These types of discrimination in effect rob a person of equal standing as a member of the society and so are utterly unacceptable: In these domains, justice demands strict equality. By contrast, the case for strict equality of *all* the factors that affect a person's economic opportunity, including gratuitous receipts, seems weak—so long as people have an adequate degree of control over their own prospects and justice in outcomes is secure.

Because of practical problems and competing values, those who regard confiscation of gratuitous receipts as an ideal will perhaps favor an actual policy not so different from this one. The theoretical gap will not yield an equally large tax policy gap. Yet some moral preference for supertaxation of such receipts will surely remain.

Even from the equal libertarian perspective, however, there is a further reason for doubting the value of higher taxation of gratuitous receipts, a reason coming from the realities of life. Inherited wealth is not the only factor that prevents equality of opportunity in a capitalist economy. Arguably more important, particularly if we take a sufficiently complex view of what makes a human life go well, is the passing on of human capital from parents to children, especially by way of educational advantages at home and at school.[45] This source of inequality is probably impossible to eliminate—short of abolishing the family—and it happens before the age at which people generally inherit.[46] Such unequal advantages are the natural result of the most basic and valuable type of interpersonal concern. But a great deal more could be done to reduce the gap by providing adequate public education for all.

Advocates of elevated wealth transfer taxation sometimes meet the point that inherited wealth is only one threat to equality of opportunity by saying that we have to start somewhere.[47] But given the importance of human capital, worsening the situation of those with inherited wealth seems unlikely to do much to improve the prospects of those with the most restricted overall opportunities.

This does not mean that there could be no grounds for an accessions tax as an addition to a scheme that adequately taxes wealth and includes gratuitous receipts in the donee's tax base. The Meade Committee Report appeals to efficiency as well as fairness as a reason for taxing inherited wealth more heavily than earned wealth. Though we take no stand on the efficiency claim, we do not believe that it would be in any sense unfair to tax inherited wealth more heavily than earnings, if this were a more efficient way to raise revenue for legitimate social purposes. We have merely rejected the idea that justice per se demands special tax treatment—or even ideally confiscation—of gratuitous receipts.

VI. Conclusion

The treatment of gratuitous receipts under the income tax, combined with the very high exemptions under the combined gift and estate tax, is an egregious injustice in the current tax scheme. There can be no justification for simply ignoring the accession of $2 million worth of inherited wealth in identifying a person's resources for the purpose of tax liability. And the situation will only get worse as the provisions of the 2001 tax legislation take effect over the next decade—to the extent that they do.

One of the worst features of the current tax system is that death is not treated as a realization event for the donor, and the tax basis of assets bequeathed is "stepped up" to fair market value at death for the purpose of the donee's capital gains tax liability, should the asset later be sold.[48] This results in complete tax forgiveness for any capital gains accrued during the decedent's lifetime. It is impossible to justify this gigantic tax break—in recent times some $30 billion in lost revenues annually—to the heirs of the rich at the expense of the great majority of taxpayers.[49] Of course, if gratuitous receipts were included in the donee's income for tax purposes, the issue would disappear, since tax would be payable on the full value of the asset. But in the absence of that more fundamental reform, the current permanent tax forgiveness of capital gains unrealized at death is an outrage.*

If gratuitous receipts were taxed to the donee under a tax scheme that taxed wealth adequately, the moral case for an additional wealth transfer tax would be fairly weak. If there is to be a separate transfer tax, however, it should take the form of a progressive accessions tax rather than a gift and estate tax levied on donors. But again, this does not mean that we support abolition of the gift and estate tax in the current nonideal situation. In the absence of the fundamental reform of including gratuitous receipts in donees' taxable income, let alone full taxation of capital gains at death, that would be a step in the direction of even greater tax injustice.[50]

Writing in 1896, the Swedish economist Knut Wicksell made a comment that is still valid:

> From [the social] point of view the main thing to do would be to take energetic measures to prevent the unearned accumulation of riches (and with it mostly also their uneconomic use) which is now encouraged by law and custom.
>
> The only practical way to reach this goal appears to me to lie in the recognition that any right of inheritance, bequest or gift necessarily involves two parts. There is the right to give and the right to receive. These must be strictly distinguished and each treated on its own merit.

---

*Simons (1938), 164–5, characterized this as "the most serious single fault" in the income tax system of his day. It may be a minor compensation, but the recent legislation that abolishes the estate tax in 2010 also introduces, starting the same year, a limit to the tax-free step-up in basis. See note 15.

To restrict the right to give more than is absolutely necessary even now often runs counter to our ideas of justice and equity and also may be seriously questioned on economic grounds.

The right of inheritance taken in the second, and more proper, sense of the word as the unlimited right to receive must, if at all, be justified in quite different terms. Unless I am much mistaken, it rests on a now obsolete conception of social and family relationships.[51]

8

Tax Discrimination

I. Justifying Differential Treatment

Most questions about the justice or fairness of the tax system, as we have emphasized, should be addressed by considering taxation as part of a more comprehensive economic picture, including expenditures for public goods and redistribution either in money or by public provision, together with the effects of all this on employment, economic growth, and the distribution of wealth and income. The broad outlines of tax policy—the identification of the tax base, the presence or absence of progressivity, the size of any general personal exemption or demogrant or tax credit for low earners—will be important aspects of the overall fiscal policy by which a society implements its conception of economic and social justice.

But because tax legislation is, in general, distinct from expenditure legislation, tax policy inevitably attracts judgments of fairness or unfairness in its own right. To some extent these judgments are based on rough assumptions about the use to which tax revenues will be put and therefore reflect more global conceptions of justice. Differences about progressivity, or about the overall level of taxes, will partly reflect differences about the importance of inequality and the legitimacy of redistribution. But there is another type of issue, more microscopic, that particularly occupies students and observers of tax policy. This is the issue of differential treatment under the tax code of different types of income or expenditure, or of persons with different characteristics or in different particular situations, even against the background of a broad pattern of unequal taxation that is taken as more or less given—or at least not subject to criticism on the same detailed grounds.

Thus, whether one thinks the income tax is too progressive, not progressive enough, or just right, it is a separate question whether the home mortgage interest deduction is fair, or the difference in treatment of the income of married couples and of unmarried persons, or the difference in treatment of capital gains and other income, to cite a few salient examples. The problem is that if the tax system, for whatever broad reasons, treats differently situated people differently, it becomes necessary to decide which are the differences that should matter. Progressivity or proportionality, deductions and exemptions are tied to the taxpayer's economic and personal situation. The question is, which differences in situation are relevant for these purposes?

The trouble with this question is that in many cases the relevance of a difference for tax purposes is mainly instrumental. That is, it has to do not with the specific characteristics of different taxpayers, but with the global effects of a tax policy that treats them differently. The decision whether to treat investment income or capital gains differently from wages, for example, would almost certainly have to be based on large-scale economic effects in regard to growth and the mobility of capital, rather than on intrinsic equity. And yet such questions are often treated in the tax policy literature under the heading of horizontal equity—as if they could be settled by direct appeal to standards of fairness.[1]

As we argued in chapters 2 and 5, the traditional idea of horizontal equity, defined as equal treatment of equals relative to some standard of vertical equity, embodies a mistake. The mistake is to take pretax income or consumption or wealth as the moral baseline and then try to formulate a standard of fairness by saying how much tax different individuals should pay as a function of their position on this baseline. The real question of fairness should be about after-tax results, not about their relation to the pretax situation. We want to know what tax schedule will raise enough money to pay for the costs of government and public services while at the same time promoting socioeconomic justice and fostering or at least not hindering a dynamic economy. That question cannot be answered by deciding in isolation who should be taxed at the same level and who should be taxed more or less. To restate the point that we have made ad nauseam: It is not a well-formed question of justice or fairness to ask, in isolation from everything else: "What function F of what variable property P of different taxpayers should determine how much each of them is taxed?" Justice is more complicated than that.

Yet it is also true that against the background of its broader aims, the details of the tax code include certain features and distinctions that are put there not for large-scale instrumental reasons but rather are carefully targeted tax breaks. Such features do invite assessment on grounds of justice. It is when a provision adds a subsidiary redistribution, in the form of a tax advantage, into the broad scheme which already serves a partly redistributive function that objections of inequity are legitimately aroused. This is not the general problem of horizontal equity but the more restricted problem of *tax discrimination*.

Any tax break is a redistribution from those who don't get it to those who do: The greater disposable income the latter are left with requires higher tax payments by the former. So the question becomes whether, in addition to redistribution from rich to poor, it is justified to redistribute from renters to homeowners, from savers to spenders, from the single to the married (or vice versa), from the young to the old, from those with children to those without, and even from the sighted to the blind.

In recent years special tax preferences designed to encourage certain expenditures and choices have proliferated. Subventions of this kind came to be known as *tax expenditures*.[2] Many of them go to businesses, to encourage invest-

ments of various kinds—for example, accelerated depreciation schedules for equipment and expensing of oil and gas
exploration costs. But individuals also benefit directly—for
example, from the exclusion from taxation of employer contributions for medical insurance and group term life insurance, and tax credits for child-care and dependent-care expenses. There are also exclusions from taxation that serve to
enhance benefits, as with Social Security, worker's compensation, and military disability pensions. Such preferences cut
across the broader profile of taxation and are often highly
selective in their impact. While they may not be unjust in
themselves, they may detract from the effectiveness of the
broader justice-seeking function of the system, if there is
one—blunting it with multiple qualifications.

Most tax advantages or disadvantages are designed to
serve some purpose other than equity. The nontaxation of
imputed rent on owner-occupied housing and the home
mortgage interest deduction promote home ownership,
which may be thought to contribute to social stability; cigarette taxes discourage smoking; tax-exempt contributions to
retirement plans encourage long-term saving and the financial independence of those past working age. Insofar as these
are legitimate goals of government, there is a case for the tax
provisions that serve them, even if they are "discriminatory."

What makes them questionable is their relation to the overall redistributive aims of the system. Cigarette taxes take a
larger proportion of the income of the poor than of the rich.
The preferential tax treatment of housing benefits homeowners
at the expense of renters; as the former are generally richer,
this too contributes to economic inequality—as well as to the
correlated economic disparities along racial and sexual lines.
And any tax deduction releases more to taxpayers in higher
brackets than in lower ones, so under a system with graduated rates, high earners realize more from the home mortgage
interest deduction and the charitable deduction than low
earners do. A tax credit for some uniform percentage of the
amount of mortgage interest payments or charitable contributions would be more equitable.

The question of fairness among taxpayers, when it comes
to these kinds of details, has to be considered against the

background of the larger aims of government that taxes serve, aims that include some form of fairness or justice in the society as a whole. Relative to such aims, a particular tax provision may be inequitable on a smaller scale if it dilutes the effect by reallocating benefits and burdens in comparison with some alternative that would serve the larger purposes of the system better by avoiding such arbitrary distinctions in treatment. This criterion permits the instrumental justification of differential treatment, since the charge of arbitrariness can often be rebutted by arguing that the distinction serves a legitimate purpose.

There is the further question, whether some distinctions in treatment are offensive even if they do further a legitimate end. Are some forms of tax discrimination just wrong in themselves, apart from their implications for economic justice or other legitimate social goals? With the exception of legally permitted affirmative action, an explicitly racial, religious, or sexual ground for differential treatment would not be allowable under our system, even if, somehow, it promoted a desirable end.[3] And a policy that introduces or worsens racial, sexual, or religious inequality (compared to a feasible alternative policy), even if this effect is not specifically intended, should be disqualified or at least subject to a higher standard of justification.[4]

II. An Example: The Marriage Penalty

We noted in chapter 2 that no tax other than a lump-sum tax can be neutral in its incentive effects with regard to all choices open to the taxpayer. A completely general requirement that the system of taxation be neutral in this way is incoherent. But there is room for a more restricted principle of tax discrimination, requiring heightened justification for any government-created economic structure whose differential impact penalizes or rewards certain types of choices, among which the state should strive to be neutral.

Such problems appear, for example, in the tax treatment of married couples, and the resulting marriage "bonuses" and marriage "penalties" under a system of progressive taxation.[5]

By examining this case, we can perhaps see more clearly what there is to the idea that certain kinds of differential impact should be avoided as unfair.

What generates political heat and political rhetoric is the current fact that when two income earners marry, their taxes often go up. In the stirring words of Representative Tillie Fowler, Republican of Florida, "What is more immoral than taxing people just because they fall in love?"[6] The trouble is that another principle of equal treatment gives rise to the problem in the present tax code: Namely, that married couples of the same total income are taxed at the same rate, however that income is divided between them. This means, under a progressive income tax with an increasing marginal rate, that unmarried taxpayers will be taxed at a higher or a lower rate than married taxpayers with the same income, or sometimes one and sometimes the other. There is an unavoidable choice between treating the single and the married equally, and treating one-earner and two-earner married couples equally; we cannot do both.[7]

The present tax law has the following consequence: The combined taxes of two single persons each earning X are less than the tax of a married couple each of whom earns X, which is equal to the tax of a married couple one of whom earns 2X and the other of whom earns nothing, which in turn is less than the tax of a single individual who earns 2X.[8] In shorthand:

$$T(X)+T(X)<T(X+X) = T(2X+0)<T(2X)$$

The first inequality is the marriage penalty and the second inequality is the marriage bonus.[9]

Is there any credible judgment of fairness to be made with regard to these equalities and inequalities, which apply at all levels of income high enough for taxes to be due?[10] There is: The idea behind them is evidently that households rather than individuals should be the taxable units, but that the distinctions between the tax rates on married couples and single individuals should not be too great in either direction. So two-earner couples are taxed somewhat more heavily than those individuals would be if they weren't married; and one-earner couples are taxed somewhat less heavily than the earner alone would be. This corresponds, presumably, to some relation among the standards of living that these different units can derive from a given level of after-tax income. The standard of living of an individual living on X will be lower, because of economies of scale, than that of a married couple living on 2X, and their standard of living will be lower, because there are two of them, than that of one individual living on 2X. This seems plausible, provided that X is not too large.

So we can see the treatment of marriage by the tax code as a kind of fine tuning of progressivity—one which tries to make differences in tax rates and after-tax income correspond to differences in standard of living of households rather than differences in income of individuals. If progressivity should correspond to standards of living, then these distinctions between the married and the unmarried may be on the whole fair, at least for incomes below the top decile. That is the argument against regarding the effects of marriage on tax liability under the present system as unfair. It is not just a penalty for falling in love.

However, this argument has been undermined by cultural developments. Today, many people fall in love and live together without getting married.* Two-earner heterosexual couples can benefit from economies of scale without incurring the marriage penalty and may therefore be deterred from marriage. One-earner same-sex couples, on the other hand, form an economic unit but can't benefit from the marriage bonus. The issue of tax discrimination is not removed by the standard-of-living defense. Whether or not exclusion of same-sex couples from legal marriage is justifiable, simply ignoring relationships other than marriage in the tax code is not. This particular objection might be remedied, however, by the recognition of "domestic partnerships" in the tax code. (That would make the joint filing bonus more widely available, but of course it wouldn't eliminate the marriage penalty.)

It is worth reemphasizing that what we are concerned with here is not that the income tax should try to avoid unequal

---

*Not to mention the dismal situation of married couples living apart.

effects on the standard of living of people whose pretax income, given their situation, would give them comparable standards of living if, impossibly, it were left entirely at their disposal. The standard of living is important, of course, but what should matter is whether the after-tax *results* are unfair, not whether these notional changes from pretax distribution are unfair.

III. Incentive Effects and Arbitrariness

The unsuitability of pretax income as a baseline is evident in another way. Unequal taxation of equal pretax incomes has an effect on incentives. It makes the same pretax income from different sources worth more or less to the income-earner and will tend to make it more expensive to attract employees or investors to the more highly taxed income-producing activity. This means that pretax income will itself be affected by choices induced by the expected level of taxation, so it would be clearly irrational to evaluate the appropriateness of that level simply by reference to the pretax income. Sometimes, as with tax-exempt municipal bonds, these incentive effects are intentional.[11] But whether they are intentional or not, it is hard to see them as in themselves unfair, unless the way they change the incentive structure has a particularly adverse effect on the options available to a class of people whose equal opportunity is a matter of social concern.

A serious example of such discriminatory effects is again provided by the relation between marriage and taxes; in this case, pretax income does not adjust to compensate for tax differentials. It is a problem having to do not with distributive justice or incentives not to marry but with incentives to work: namely, the effect of joint filing on the compensation after taxes of second earners, who in the present state of society tend to be women. (A second earner is a spouse whose employment is optional rather than mandatory.) If it is taken as given that the husband will work for pay, the wife's decision to work will be made on the basis that the whole of her salary will be taxed at their marginal rate—meaning that the reward in spendable income will be much less than for his salary, which would benefit from both their personal exemptions, any dependent deductions, and perhaps a lower marginal rate.[12] If we add the cost of child care to make it possible for her to go out to work, it's even worse—a good reason for the child-care tax credit.

These differential incentives matter from the standpoint of justice because they so massively reinforce the division of labor within the family that is associated with the inferior status of women in society as a whole. Even women who would like to work outside the home are deterred from doing so because the higher tax burden for second earners makes domestic work economically preferable. This is a problem of sexual rather than distributive justice, though it fits under the broader category of equality of opportunity. It could be ameliorated by switching to a system of purely individual taxation, but that, of course, would undermine the equivalence of treatment of one-earner and two-earner couples with the same total income. Perhaps it is time to recognize this as an equivalence with a sexist bias. It seems likely that different effects on men and women, mediated by differences in their social roles, provide serious examples of objectionable tax discrimination, and that the subject merits continued scrutiny.[13]

Every tax that is not, like a head tax, simply assessed on everyone independent of what they do will have some motivational consequences for people's choices, some "distorting effect." A modern tax system cannot hope to be neutral in its incentive effects with regard to people's economically significant decisions about work, leisure, consumption, ownership, and form of life. If there are requirements of neutrality, they must be rather special and related to fundamental matters like sex, race, or religion. There would be nothing unfair, for example, in a tax on chocolate ice cream but not on vanilla, though it would be arbitrary.

Yet the general concern over nonneutrality persists and even provides the basis for disagreement over such fundamental tax reform questions as whether the income tax should be replaced with a consumption tax. As we said in chapter 5, there are serious arguments that might be made in favor of such a change. But we also tried to explain why the discrimination against savers taken by itself is a spurious moral issue—about as serious as would be the issue of discrimination against childless couples by the dependent exemption.

Likewise, the home mortgage interest deduction, and the nontaxability of imputed rent of owner-occupied housing, are often said to discriminate against renters. But these are not morally interesting categories.* Whether the mortgage deduction is a good idea depends on whether the loss of revenue and consequent need for higher taxes elsewhere is compensated by the social desirability of widespread home ownership for relatively young families. The aspect of the mortgage deduction that seems most probably unwarranted is its extension to second homes.

But the general point is that we cannot decide whether a tax preference is unfair by examining it in isolation. We have to decide (a) whether it distorts the broader pattern of redistribution and financing of public provision that our general conception of justice requires, by shifting some of the costs or by surreptitiously diminishing or increasing the amount of redistribution; (b) whether it serves other purposes, legitimate for fiscal policy, which are important enough to override any such shortfall.

Against a generally legitimate background, any deduction or exemption could in principle pose the question of fairness. A deliberately targeted tax break or tax expenditure is likely to involve distortion of the broader redistributive aims of the system; unfortunately, this method of supporting desired activities has become increasingly common, as a replacement for direct appropriations. Political leverage often has a lot to do with it, and such wrinkles are apt to be somewhat arbitrary. But the usual methods of identifying violations of horizontal equity are not a reliable guide. Deviations from pretax equivalence do not as such merit strict scrutiny.

What should replace the norm of horizontal equity is that of avoiding morally objectionable or objectionably caused

---

*By contrast, the argument that the current tax treatment of housing has a racially discriminatory impact must be taken seriously; see Moran and Whitford (1996).

inequality in the system of property of which taxes form an essential part. What is objectionable will depend on different theories of justice and may have partly to do with the resulting profile of standards of living, partly with the influence of causes that are beyond people's control, and partly with the absence of causes that *are* under their control, which would give them more responsibility. Whether a particular tax preference or loophole or exemption is unfair should be determined by whether it undermines the capacity of the system to promote the broader aims of justice in the society, however they are interpreted. But for the most part, we believe that horizontal equity as traditionally conceived, by comparison with a mythical no-tax world, should cease to be regarded as a significant issue for justice in taxation.

9

Conclusion: Politics

I. Theory and Practice

Our main message throughout this book has been that societal fairness, rather than tax fairness, should be the value that guides tax policy, and that property rights are conventional: they are to a large extent the product of tax policies that have to be evaluated by standards of social justice; so they cannot be used to determine what taxes are just.

But there is a big distance between evaluative and theoretical claims like these and the determination of taxes in the real world. Public policy is not made by philosopher kings. In a democracy it is made by political representatives subject to removal by their constituents, and realistic grounds for action have to recognize the complicated dynamics of this mechanism. Pure reflection on what would be just has its place in the discussion of public policy and is the main task of moral and political philosophy. But it is a long way from the description of such an ideal to its enactment or even influence; and if the ideal involves the criticism of ingrained conceptions so unconscious that they seem natural, the obstacles are formidable. In addition, the appeal to justice is only one motive in political debate, and by no means the most powerful. All this brings us to the further question, what politically feasible results might be drawn from the foregoing reflections, and what mixture of motives in the pluralistic electorate of a modern capitalist democracy might be called on in support of just and viable tax policies?*

The widening of the angle of vision from tax justice to social justice is less of a departure from ordinary politics than it is from traditional tax policy analysis. It is true that recent political debates have made the traditional questions of horizontal equity, which focus narrowly on the distribution of tax burdens, much more salient to the public imagination. But usually, when fairness is an issue with regard to the tax system in popular debate, it is related to differences over steep economic inequality, individual responsibility, the alleviation of poverty, equality of opportunity, universal guarantees of basic social protection, and the sharing out of the cost of government and other public goods.

Much of our discussion of the relation between tax policy and current issues of political theory fits into those debates and tries to clarify them by setting out and distinguishing the possible positions more precisely. We have talked about the different kinds of results that holders of different conceptions of justice would want the tax system to aim at; why people disagree about the fairness of leaving large gains in the hands of those who do well out of the capitalist economy and their descendants; and also about the desirability of public guarantees by the state of a significant social minimum. Even though programs like Social Security and Medicare are now unassailable in the political mainstream of American society, the extent and financing of such provision is very much under debate. Recognizably philosophical questions about our responsibilities for ourselves and for one another are central to the political conflicts here.

Where our approach departs greatly from the standard mentality of day-to-day politics is in our insistence on the

---

*We leave aside an important practical constraint that applies less to the United States than to other countries: the pressure international financial markets exert on economic policy, including tax policy. The only solution to this problem would seem to lie with international economic institutions.

conventionality of property, and our denial that property rights are morally fundamental. Resistance to traditional concepts of tax fairness and their political analogues requires rejection of the idea that people's pretax income and wealth are theirs in any morally meaningful sense. We have to think of property as what is created by the tax system, rather than what is disturbed or encroached on by the tax system. Property rights are the rights people have in the resources they are entitled to control after taxes, not before.

This doesn't mean we can't speak of taking money by taxation from the rich to give to the poor, for example. But what that means is not that we are taking from some people what is already theirs, but rather that the tax system is assigning to them less that counts as theirs than they would have under a less redistributive system that left the rich with more money under their private control, that is, with more that is theirs.

This shift to a purely conventional conception of property is, we acknowledge, counterintuitive. Taxes are naturally perceived by most people as expropriations of their property—taking from them some of what is originally theirs and using it for various purposes determined by the government. Most people, we assume, instinctively think of their pretax income as theirs until the government takes it away from them, and also think the same way about other people's earnings and wealth. Political rhetoric picks up on this natural way of thinking: "You know better what to do with your money than the government does." "The surplus doesn't belong to the government; it belongs to the people."

Changing this habit of thought would require a kind of gestalt shift, and it may be unrealistic to hope that such a shift in perception could easily become widespread. It isn't that people are unwilling to pay taxes, but they tend to think of taxes as an incursion by the government on a prior distribution of property and income by reference to which expropriation and redistribution has to be justified. That question has the form: "How much of what is mine should be taken from me to support public services or to be given to others? How much of what others possess should be taken from them and given to me?" Whereas we have been arguing that the right question is: "How should the tax system divide the social product between the private control of individuals and government control, and what factors should it cause or permit to determine who ends up with what?"

As we have seen, putting the question this way still leaves room for radical disagreement about the answer, but it is likely to arouse strong resistance nonetheless. It sounds too much like the claim that the entire social product really belongs to the government, and that all after-tax income should be seen as a kind of dole that each of us receives from the government, if it chooses to look on us with favor. To this the natural indignant response would be that just because we are all subjects of the same state, it doesn't follow that we collectively own each other, together with our productive contributions.

But there is a misperception here. It is true that we don't own each other, but the correct place for this observation is in the context of an argument over the form of a system of property rights that gives due weight to individual freedom and responsibility. It doesn't justify starting with pretax income—over which individuals *couldn't, as a matter of logic*, be given full private control—as the baseline from which departures must be justified.

The state does not own its citizens, nor do they own each other collectively. But individual citizens don't own anything except through laws that are enacted and enforced by the state. Therefore, the issues of taxation are not about how the state should appropriate and distribute what its citizens already own, but about how it should allow ownership to be determined.

We recognize that it is a lot to hope that this philosophical point should become psychologically real to most people. Pretax economic transactions are so salient in our lives that the governmental framework that determines their consequences and gives them their real meaning recedes into the background of consciousness. What is left is the robust and compelling fantasy that we earn our income and the government takes some of it away from us, or in some cases supplements it with what it has taken from others. This results in widespread hostility to taxes, and a political advantage to those who campaign against them and attack the IRS as a tyrannical bureaucracy, trying to get its hands on our hard-earned money.

If political debate were not over how much of what is mine the government should take in taxes, but over how the laws, including the tax system, should determine what is to count as mine, it would not end disagreements over the merits of redistribution and public provision, but it would change their form. The question would become what values we want to uphold and reflect in our collectively enacted system of property rights—how much weight should be given to the alleviation of poverty and the provision of equal chances; how much to ensuring that people reap the rewards and penalties for their efforts or lack thereof; how much to leaving people free of interference in their voluntary interactions. It is not ruled out that the preferred system would be one that denied the state substantial responsibility for combating economic inequality; but that position could not rely on the support of pretax property rights.

The difficulty of trying to produce such a shift to a conventionalist mentality is that people are rightly jealous of their property rights in what is genuinely theirs—what the law puts under their discretionary control—and these possessive sentiments don't naturally restrict themselves within the boundaries of after-tax resources, which seem too abstract. In fact, it is pretax income that is an abstraction, but those are the numbers that wage or salary earners are most familiar with. It would not be easy to displace the feeling that they represent the starting point from which taxes are a departure, and that poses an obstacle to the political influence of many theories of justice.

II. Justice and Self-Interest

There is a completely different way of seeing the political debate, however, which may be still more significant. So far we have been talking about social justice and different ways of conceiving of it. But it is fairly clear to the most casual observer of the American scene that the predominant motive determining political choice by citizens and the motive principally addressed by the rhetoric of politicians, especially when they talk about taxes, is individual self-interest. There may even be nothing wrong with this from the point of view of certain theories of political legitimacy, according to which the point of the democratic process is to arrive at collective decisions by pooling individual interests and balancing them against one another. But if that is the case, what is the point of trying to inject explicit considerations of justice into the debate?

We believe this view of politics and political legitimacy is too simple. Appeals to justice are everywhere mixed with appeals to self-interest, in politics and in the minds of individuals—even if self-interest predominates. The political case for tax cuts disproportionately benefiting the rich, presented to the American people at the start of the second Bush administration, would be much less compelling if it could not be presented as an issue of fairness. It's one thing to say, "this will be good for most people, especially the rich, that's why I am in favor of it," and quite another to say, "it's only fair that everybody should get a tax break." Even if such talk is disingenuous, it does connect up with long-standing conceptions of tax fairness that have significant appeal.[1] No progress can be made at the political level without taking such conceptions of justice in taxation seriously, subjecting them to criticism, and proposing an alternative. Nevertheless, the basic question survives, because the motives of justice and self-interest may not point in the same direction, either for individuals or for groups, and the process of finding an accommodation between them poses some of the hardest problems of ethics, political theory, and practical politics.

Individuals in a capitalist economy pursue their economic self-interest in the market, both as buyers and as sellers of labor and other goods. It is economic self-interest that largely determines the way they respond to the tax laws—making choices, when they can, in order to reduce their tax burden or increase their after-tax revenue. Why then should we not expect each of them to favor general tax policies on the basis of what is best for them, economically, as individuals? This will not necessarily be the policy that taxes them least, since most people recognize that they benefit from some government activities that must be financed by taxes. But it would probably mean that each citizen or group would favor a system that minimized their share of total taxes, and that the haves would strongly resist tax-based transfers of income to the have-nots, while the poor would clamor for higher taxes on the rich.

To some extent this is what happens in politics, with politicians situating themselves to the right or left of center by appealing to these different interests. But if this were all, then tax policy debate would leave no place for questions of fairness or justice. It would be simply a contest for votes based on self-interest. In the United States, it would be complicated by the direct influence of money on political campaigns, which means that those who can afford to contribute heavily to politicians find their interests more closely attended to than those who cannot, and gain an advantage in the legislative contest out of proportion to their numbers— with respect both to who is elected and to what tax policies they favor. All this is familiar from recent U.S. politics, where the issue of lower taxes is hotly contested.

But in spite of the importance of money and the straight conflict of economic interests, we think it would be excessively cynical to conclude that this is all that is happening. United States politics is also rife with appeals to what is right, and they are not necessarily all hypocritical rationalizations, even if many of them are. Some well-off people favor redistributive policies that would leave them with less wealth than they might otherwise end up with;[2] others argue that reduced taxes on the rich are better for everyone, because of trickle-down effects; and some poorer people are opposed to soaking the rich, and believe in abolition of the estate tax. In other words, although people's political choices are certainly motivated at least in part by self-interest, most also admit some weight to moral arguments: They want to be able to represent their political preferences to themselves and to others as right or justified—as acceptable from a point of view that takes the interests of all members of the society properly into account.

The big question for anyone interested in the implementation of normative principles of justice in taxation is how much tension between the motive of economic self-interest and the motive of justice voters can be expected to tolerate. Is it realistic, in other words, to propose on grounds of justice a policy that can win politically only if it is supported by significant numbers of citizens who would be left economically better off under a different policy? This question has particular force in regard to redistributive measures that pay special attention to the poor, who form a minority in our society; but it could also be asked about antiredistributive policies that favor the rich at the expense of the middle and lower classes, on libertarian grounds.

In the United States, with its single-member constituencies and its two-party winner-take-all presidential election, politicians have given a clear answer to this question: You may use moral arguments, but you have to present your policies as being in the individual interest of most of the electors. And even if your aim is to combat inequality, the most politically viable programs for this purpose are those that can be presented as serving *everyone's* interests. Even if they are in fact redistributive through their financing, programs like Social Security and Medicare, which can fudge this feature, create a constituency so broad that it makes them almost unassailable.

It may therefore be the case that even those whose utilitarian or egalitarian ideals would be best served by a system that gave priority to lifting the standard of living and opportunities of people at the bottom of the social heap should seek concrete policies that provide benefits to everyone—even if they do less for the worst off than ideal alternatives that require too much moral motivation. The sense of solidarity with those economically less well-off is too weak in our society to win elections, though it can be appealed to as a supplement to the basic political diet of collective self-interest.

There may be a limit, in other words, to the degree to which people in a capitalist society or any other can be expected to separate their political from their private motives. (Whether the limit is merely psychological or whether it is also morally justified is a question we leave aside.) Some separation is certainly possible, and indeed essential for the general sense of legitimacy in democratic government. Statesmen have the responsibility to evoke public motives by appealing to decency as well as greed. But experience suggests that we should not expect too much. Politicians are always most comfortable when appeals to self-interest and to moral rectitude can be made out to coincide.

III. Plausible Policies

We have tried to present the significant rival positions on social and economic justice, but we have not concealed our own views about the region in which the truth lies. While we don't hold the same views about foundational questions of moral and political theory,[3] we are in rough agreement about what a tax system should aim at. In this section we will say something about the policies that seem to us plausible as means to those aims, taking into account the conditions of political viability discussed in the previous sections.

We believe that the main problem of socioeconomic justice is this. A capitalist market economy is the best method we have for creating employment, generating wealth, allocating capital to production, and distributing goods and services. But it also inevitably generates large economic and social inequalities, often hereditary, that leave a significant segment of society not only relatively but also absolutely deprived, unless special measures are taken to combat those effects. Our view is that while every government has the fundamental duty to guarantee security against coercion and violence, both foreign and domestic, and to provide the legal order that makes prosperity possible, it is almost as important to find ways of limiting the damage to the inevitable losers in market competition without undermining the productive power of the system.

It isn't possible to ensure that everyone will have exactly the same chances in life. The most realistic aim is to try to ensure that everyone in the society should have at least a minimally decent quality of life—that none should start out with two strikes against them because of low-earning capacity, poor education, a severely deprived childhood and home environment, inadequate food, shelter, and medical care; and that even people who fail to take advantage of reasonably favorable initial opportunities should not be left to fall into destitution. Preventing or compensating for those harms is overwhelmingly more important than attacking inequalities at the upper end of the distribution. It is the fundamental positive responsibility we have toward our fellow citizens.

Any view more laissez-faire than this depends on the moral belief that the only positive obligations of government are: (a) to provide institutions that make a market economy possible, (b) to protect people from violence and coercion, and (c) to supply certain public goods that serve everyone's interests but cannot be provided privately. We have explained why we reject the everyday libertarianism that lies behind such a view. Without that support it seems arbitrarily restrictive: Why just those positive obligations and not also the obligation to ensure a minimally decent standard of living for all citizens? The idea that it is the function of government merely to provide the conditions for peaceful economic cooperation and competition, without any concern for the equity of the results, is just too minimal. On the other hand, while we are sympathetic to more robust egalitarian views that take social responsibility substantially beyond the level of minimal decency, their political prospects seem dim, at least in the short run.

It goes without saying that exemption from tax for a minimum basic income would be one element in the institutional scheme that ensures a decent social minimum; but the most effective way of improving the condition of people below the average would be not only to exempt them from tax but also to substantially increase their disposable income. The difficulty is to come up with methods of doing this that really work and don't have seriously objectionable effects of other kinds.[4] The perennial debate about rises in the minimum wage provides an example; it seems likely that this is a measure that could achieve only modest improvement in the income of those with the least marketable skills, because large increases would be too damaging economically.

We believe that direct cash transfers are a better method, and that the hard question is how they could be designed so as not to deter recipients from paid work. The importance of this issue cannot be exaggerated. Remunerated and productive work, by at least someone in the family, is a vital condition of self-respect, stability, independence, and a sense of social membership. Cash transfers that provide disincentives to work are socially destructive.

On the other hand, transfers to those who cannot work or who have passed the age when they are expected to work do not have the same disadvantage. That is why Social Security benefits are unproblematic. They protect everyone in the society from falling through a certain floor in old age, and while they provide some disincentive to go on working forever in this age of no compulsory retirement, they do not discourage work by anyone whom the society should want to keep in employment. While the fact is somewhat disguised by the Social Security taxes that all workers pay, and the benefits that are a function of contribution, the program is clearly redistributive: low earners get back more than they put in, and high earners less.

But a program of cash transfers to those of working age, even if it is targeted partly at the support of children too young to work, ought to take a form that encourages work and doesn't lower the gains from employment or lead to the breakup of households, in the way that some welfare programs can. Tax-supported wage supplements channeled through employers would be one way to do this; we will not try to evaluate that method here.[5] In Europe, direct grants in the form of family allowances are common, providing some support to every family with children. Clearly, there are political advantages to such a universal program, and if it could be financed in a redistributive way, it would do a lot to correct the current skewing of entitlement programs toward the old, through Social Security and Medicare.

But a more targeted, need-based form of income supplement has been tried with some success in the United States: the Earned Income Tax Credit, which is worth 40% of income up to $8,890 per year for a family with two children.[6] This kind of direct benefit to the working poor—those who lose out in a competitive labor market, whose intrinsic inequalities are now widely recognized—seems to have gained mainstream political acceptance. It has appeal both for enemies of inequality and for those champions of individual responsibility who recognize that low-earning power need not be the victim's fault.

It is hard to know how much more extensive, either in amount or in range of recipients, such programs of direct income supplement could realistically hope to become. Our guess is that a targeted program of cash transfers would lose all political viability if it went above the bottom quarter of the income distribution, and that a serious effort to guarantee a decent social minimum would probably have to take the alternative form of universal benefits, funded in a redistributive way. A family allowance is something that may take hold in the United States eventually. If so, the currently dim prospects for general acceptance of demogrants might even improve.

More specific programs like universal health insurance and adequate funding for public education in all communities are also necessary parts of any fully adequate social safety net. If some such measures were added to Social Security, Medicare, and the existing public support for educational opportunity, it would be a significant move toward social justice as we understand it. But we recognize that there is much more resistance to direct public provision of social benefits—"big government"—here than in other rich countries, so it seems particularly desirable to expand the redistribution of disposable cash through the tax system, which does not involve the creation of government-run programs.

Turning to the question of revenue, we will now review how we come down on some issues discussed extensively in three earlier chapters: the tax base, progressivity, and the inheritance of wealth. Again, we believe that tax policy should be dictated not by a narrow focus on the allocation of tax burdens but by the joint aims of financing public goods at the right level and securing social justice; and the latter, in our view, requires an attempt to protect the lives and opportunities of individuals and families who have fared poorly in the capitalist economy, without undermining its creative power.

The first of these aims, the financing of public goods, was discussed in chapter 4. We argued there that, even without any reference to principles that require the reduction of socioeconomic inequality or special consideration for the worst off, public goods should be financed by unequal contributions from citizens with unequal resources. This is true simply because we should want the level of provision of public goods to reflect their value to citizens by comparison with alternative private uses of the same resources, and that value is different in monetary terms depending on how much resources each citizen has. By itself this does not tell us how taxation for public goods should vary with income, except that it should be a positive function. But our sense of the steepness of the rate at which the marginal utility of private money diminishes suggests to us that this factor alone provides a significant prima facie case for progressivity, in addition to the egalitarian reasons that we ourselves would also accept.

How much progressivity there should be, and of what form, turns not only on issues of social justice but also on complex empirical factors; it is therefore a question on which we have no firm opinion. The progressivity of net taxes that comes from a substantial personal exemption, perhaps coupled with some form of negative income tax or even a demogrant, seems to be clearly indicated as part of any just system. What is unclear is the appropriate progressivity or lack thereof in marginal tax rates.

We have expressed doubt that optimal tax theory will ultimately justify declining marginal rates. For primary earners, there is no evidence for a significant adverse effect of increasing marginal rates on hours worked, at least if they don't become confiscatory.[7] Similarly, the influence of tax rates on the overall rate of saving appears to be negligible or nonexistent.[8] In respect to labor supply and overall levels of investment, then, the trickle-down theory is not empirically confirmed. As explained in chapter 6, taxable income does appear to be more responsive to after-tax returns, but this behavioral effect itself depends for its possibility on the tax laws and is not a brute fact that economic policy must accommodate: Just how significant the effect is or should be is itself largely a matter for policymakers to determine, just like the optimal demogrant and rate structure.[9] However, one reason against taxing high earners heavily at the margin seems to have been established, namely, that the entrepreneurs among them appear to be deterred from investment outlays by high income tax rates.[10] Here the supply-side outlook evidently has some weight.

On the other hand, when it comes to the choice of tax base, we are not persuaded that the exemption of capital income through a move to a consumption tax is warranted. If we are serious about redistribution, income (or consumption plus wealth) remains the appropriate tax base, mainly because that's where the money is. Increases in wealth, including entrepreneurial wealth, are a very important part of the income of the upper segments of the economic distribution, and income taxes rather than wealth or accessions taxes seem the most politically practicable means of taxing them.* It is unrealistic to think that all the tax revenue left untouched by a pure consumption tax could be effectively recaptured by a politically feasible accessions tax.

Two of the practical issues of tax policy—progressivity and inheritance taxes—are connected with another question of justice. That is the question of whether large inequalities toward the top of the economic distribution are objectionable, independently of the value of lifting the standard of living and opportunities of those toward the bottom. The political and moral climate in the United States is not currently hostile to huge salaries and huge accumulations of wealth, as such, and there is not even much concern over the intergenerational transmission of these fortunes. Public opinion seems to take the view that capitalism at its most successful will inevitably generate large upward inequalities, and that, in themselves, they don't do much harm. In any event, the tolerance for vast private wealth is a natural response to the sense of its inevitability.

We are uncertain about this question. There is something palpably unfair about a society in which a small minority are vastly richer than their compatriots, and in which successive

---

*We leave aside the much debated question whether capital gains should be taxed at the same rate as other income. A proper investigation of this question requires attention also to the role of the corporate income tax, a topic we have not addressed.

generations are born into these positions of wealth, even if no one in the society is very badly off in absolute terms. Clearly, a significant part of this good fortune is undeserved. But we don't know how much this matters—whether it is bad, in particular, for the less-privileged members of the society to live in such an unequal situation. Probably comparing yourself with people slightly above you is more painful than contemplating those in the economic stratosphere. In any case, fantastic good luck that is undeserved is in itself nothing to object to. And bringing down the top, unless it is a means of bringing up the rest, is not a policy that can be easily defended by politically attractive arguments.

But we also firmly reject the opposite view that economic winners morally deserve to keep their big gains and to pass them on to their children. Something like this view seems to underlie the hostility to estate and gift taxes, even for the very rich, that is increasingly common in our society. The broad support for abolition of all taxes on estates cannot express merely the self-interest of those in the top economic tier, since under the present combined estate and gift tax only a small minority of bequests are subject to tax at all.

Taxation of large family fortunes at death should certainly be regarded as a legitimate source of revenue for redistribution and other purposes, and it should be politically possible to make the case that this is not a violation of a moral entitlement or natural property right based on justice. As we argue in chapter 7, the strongest case can be made for including bequests in the taxable income of the recipient. But even if the only politically viable option is to continue to tax bequests to the donor in a separate estate and gift tax, eliminating this source of revenue would be a clear step toward greater injustice.

Finally, any policy proposals that reduce the after-tax disposable resources of the wealthy have to contend with the importance of money in American politics. People will spend money, where they can, to gain or retain still more money. If political contributions are not limited, we can expect the pursuit of socioeconomic justice to be handicapped by the disproportionate influence of those who have the most to lose from it financially. Fortunately, this is now widely appreciated, and there is a serious movement for campaign finance reform. The same forces that make such reform necessary will make it difficult to enact. But if limits on campaign spending become law and are judged constitutional, one significant injustice resulting from large concentrations of wealth will have been eliminated.

IV. Effective Moral Ideas

Nothing could be more mundane than taxes, but they provide a perfect setting for constant moral argument and possible moral progress. Progress in moral thinking is slow, and effective progress cannot come exclusively from theoreticians, as it can in mathematics, for example. In mathematics, everyone else is content to trust the experts, but when it comes to justice, a new conception or argument will not acquire authority until many people take it into their own thinking and come to be motivated by it in their judgments of what to do and what to favor or oppose.

We see how long moral changes can take by looking back on the abolition of slavery, the growth of democracy, and the public recognition of full sexual and racial equality. What is obvious to us was once far from obvious to many people—though there have always been individuals morally in advance of their time (as well, of course, as people who remain behind).

The development of a conception of justice compatible with capitalism and realizable under democracy is a formidable intellectual task. It would require more than simply letting the demands of justice yield to pressure from the other two. But the spread of such a conception so that it becomes part of the habit of thought of most of those who live in the capitalist liberal democracies is a problem of a different kind. The moral ideas that do the work of legitimation have to be graspable and intuitively appealing, not just correct.

In the aftermath of the century during which the Marxist conception of equality played itself out, at enormous cost, the question is whether a different kind of egalitarian social ideal, one not intrinsically incompatible with capitalist economic institutions, can take hold in the Western democracies that are now firmly committed both to democracy and to capitalism, with its inevitably unequal distribution of income and wealth. This would have to be a replacement for the old capitalist conception of responsibility for human welfare in terms of charity, understood as a morally motivated personal gift from the fortunate to the unfortunate—replacement by an understanding that legal institutions define who owns what and that those institutions must satisfy independent standards of distributive justice.

We believe that there is hope in this direction from the increasingly widespread understanding of how capitalism works—the gradual increase of popular economic literacy in democratic societies. The ways in which people can be both the beneficiaries and the victims of the market, and the respects in which it does and does not provide opportunities for individuals to enrich themselves through contributions to investment and production, are increasingly understood by the general public.

The egalitarian attitude that has a chance of taking hold against this background is the idea that in a pure labor market poverty may be nobody's fault, and that if wages are set at what the market will bear, significant numbers of people will not earn enough to maintain a decent standard of living. These inequalities, generated by a system that benefits most people substantially and some people spectacularly, should come to be seen as unacceptable properties of the system, requiring rectification by some form of publicly financed social minimum—either in cash or in public provision. This is close to the moderate social democratic ideal that is a significant element of opinion in contemporary Europe, and there is no reason why it should not become part of the everyday moral consensus of Western politics. If so, more robust egalitarian views could begin to be treated as falling within the range of reasonable political opinion, even in the United States.

The older equalities had to be won against ancient traditions of exclusion—by hereditary rank, by religion, by race, or by sex. Those victories are embodied in recognized rights that confer a common legal and political status on all members of the society. Nothing so simple will do for the expression of an egalitarian socioeconomic ideal in the context of capitalism. But the acceptance of socioeconomic inequality as inevitable can coexist with an insistence that those who do worst out of our common system should not fare too badly, and that those who do well out of it have no cause for complaint if the universal guarantee of a decent social minimum leaves them with less than they would have if low earners were left in poverty.

We may hope that in spite of the decisive failure of public ownership of the means of production in the twentieth century, most people are coming to believe that even under capitalism the organization of the economy, and the allocation of its product between public and private control, is a legitimate object of continual collective choice, and that this choice must be made on grounds that justify it not only economically but morally, and by a democratic procedure that legitimizes it. There will always be room for disagreement over the values that should determine that choice. But at least such an outlook provides a clear place for the application of standards of justice to tax policy and a role for the philosophical pursuit of disagreements among them.

Notes

CHAPTER ONE

1. See Aristotle's *Politics*, bk. 1, ch. 5.

CHAPTER TWO

1. For a historical account of the political morality strand of tax policy analysis up to the end of the nineteenth century, see Seligman (1908).

2. Sometimes simplicity is offered as a distinct criterion; we treat it as an aspect of efficiency, broadly understood.

3. That justice in taxation consists in a fair distribution of tax burdens seems still to be the dominant view of public finance economists; see, e.g., Slemrod and Bakija (2000), chap. 3; Bradford (1986), chap. 8; Stiglitz (2000), chap. 17. It is also taken for granted in polemical texts such as Hall and Rabushka (1995).

But this approach has also come in for strong criticism, at least since the late nineteenth century; see Wicksell (1896). For more recent works, see, e.g., Gordon (1972); Bankman and Griffith (1987); Griffith (1993); Kornhauser (1996a); Fried (1999a).

See also Kaplow (1989, 1995a, and forthcoming). While we agree with Kaplow that traditional tax equity norms ought to be abandoned, we do not accept his argument that utilitarianism, or some other weighted measure of total individual welfare, should be the sole guide in tax policy. Kaplow has recently extended his defense of welfarism to cover all areas of public policy; see Kaplow and Shavell (2001). As the next chapter will make clear, while we agree with Kaplow and Shavell that overall social outcomes are very important, we do not share their view that the only relevant consideration for the assessment of a legal rule or social policy is its effect on individuals' welfare.

4. See Musgrave (1959), 160.

5. Schoenblum (1995) is, as he acknowledges (270), a very rare exception. And even he advocates an exemption for low income earners (270–1).

The British government's attempt, in 1990, to introduce a head tax in even the limited sphere of local government led to violent riots and is commonly thought to have played a role in Margaret Thatcher's downfall as prime minister.

6. For a general discussion of the idea of relevant differences, see Hart (1994), 158–63.

7. See Graetz (1995), 63–8, criticizing Joint Committee on Taxation (1993).

8. See the essays in Bradford (1995); these tables are prepared by the professional staffs of the Treasury Department, the Congressional Joint Committee on Taxation, and the Congressional Budget Office.

9. See Graetz (1995), 65–6. What typically is included in the tables is the Earned-Income Tax Credit (EITC). Graetz writes that the "most likely explanation for this practice is that EITC outlays are governed by a provision of the Internal Revenue code, rather than other titles of the U.S. code" (66–7).

10. Bradford (1995), 3.

11. This is the conclusion Graetz reaches in the course of his critique of the use of distribution tables. He recommends that tax schemes should be assessed by reference to their impact on the post-tax distribution of income; see Graetz (1995), 30.

12. Over the course of its history, appeal to the benefits of government has been put to two very different uses. In the hands of its early advocates, a distinguished group including Grotius, Pufendorf, Hobbes, Locke, Rousseau, and Smith (Seligman [1908], 158–204; Musgrave [1959], 61–8), the benefit principle was understood as addressing the problem of the fair distribution of tax burdens—the problem before us in this chapter. This use of the principle continued through the twentieth century; see, e.g., Hayek (1960), 315–16. But starting in the late nineteenth century, economists began invoking benefits in a more restricted way to approach

a different problem, that of determining the proper scope of public as opposed to private provision—what benefits the government should provide directly and at what level. We discuss this second type of benefit principle in chapter 4. For an overview of the two types of benefit principle, with a clear account of the difference between them, see Musgrave (1959), chap. 4.

13. See Gibbard (1991). This point is not undermined by the possibility of cooperation for mutual protection in the state of nature— for such is the road to government; see Nozick (1974), chap. 2.

14. This conclusion has often been drawn. See, e.g., Hayek (1960), 315-16. For a general discussion of the argument from the benefit principle to proportionate taxation, see Fried (1999a).

15. Fried (1999a) discusses a quite different interpretation of the benefit principle (understood as a principle of justice in taxation): Taxes are to be understood as the prices paid for government services, such that, as in the private market, it is quite irrelevant both how much utility a person derives from consuming a given quantity of government services and how much disutility is occasioned by paying a certain dollar amount in tax; people should pay dollar amounts in proportion to the quantity of services consumed. But as she herself so convincingly shows, it is not at all clear what argument of justice might lie behind the view that taxes should be seen as "shadow" prices for government "services." Blum and Kalven (1952), 454, refer to "the well worn rhetorical question: Since the rich and the poor pay at the same rate for bread, why shouldn't they pay at the same rate in buying government?" But this is indeed just rhetoric, since government is not, in fact, a commodity for sale. If there is a reason for thinking that justice will be served by thinking of government *as if* it were a commodity for sale, we need to know what that reason is. Fried reconstructs some arguments on behalf of this view; we agree with her rejection of them. The more traditional interpretation of the benefit principle (as a principle of justice in taxation) rests, by contrast, on a simple and compelling intuition: People should be burdened by taxes in proportion to the benefits they receive from what taxes make possible.

It may well be that the proper division of public and private provision can be determined by thinking of government services as if they were commodities whose supply should be determined by demand. But this, as already indicated (see note 12), is a quite different issue from that of the equitable division of tax burdens generally.

16. The benefit principle as interpreted here requires, in effect, that people be burdened by taxation in proportion to their welfare;

it is thus in practice equivalent to the principle that taxes should exact the same proportional sacrifice of welfare from each person (discussed further in section VI below). It has been shown that such a criterion may lead to progressive, proportionate, or regressive taxation, depending on the way in which marginal utility of income declines. For a succinct account, with references, see Musgrave (1959), 100–102.

17. Even the "end of welfare" U.S. Personal Responsibility and Work Opportunity Reconciliation Act of 1996 leaves in place food stamps and Medicaid; for an account of the changes introduced by this act, see Hershkoff and Loffredo (1997); for ongoing reports on its effects, see the website of the Urban Institute: http://www.urban.org/news/focus/focus_welfare.html (last visited May 30, 2001).

18. Again, we are talking about the general form of the benefit principle, based on the total benefit from government—not the restricted form in which it is used to determine the appropriate level of provision of public goods. See note 12 and chap. 4.

19. See Vanistendael (1996), 22–4.

20. See, e.g., Mirrlees (1986), 1197–8, 1209–17; Atkinson and Stiglitz (1980), 356–62.

21. For the history of the idea of ability to pay, see Seligman (1908), 204–89; Kiesling (1992), chap. 2.

22. See Walker (1888), 14–16. For a recent endorsement of this interpretation of ability to pay, see Bradford (1986), chap. 8.

23. See also chapter 5, note 67.

24. Bradford being a notable exception; see note 22.

25. We ignore here the differences between utilitarian political theory and the assumptions of welfare economics. For discussion, see, e.g., Atkinson and Stiglitz (1980), 333–65; see also chapter 3, section V.

26. See, e.g., Tuomala (1990), 51–7; Stiglitz (1987), 993–6.

27. See Mill (1871), bk. 5, chap. 2.

28. Blum and Kalven (1952), 517.

29. Pigou (1947), 44.

30. See, e.g., Musgrave and Musgrave (1989), 228–31. For discussion, see Musgrave (1959), 95–8; Blum and Kalven (1952), 455–71; Fried (1998), 153–5. An early defender of the principle of equal proportional sacrifice was the Dutch economist A. J. Cohen-Stuart; see Musgrave (1959), 98. An early defense of the principle of equal marginal sacrifice is Edgeworth (1897).

31. As Edgeworth (1897) makes clear. The principle of equal marginal sacrifice requires that the last dollar paid in tax by each

person exact the same real sacrifice. If the marginal value of income diminishes for all monetary increments, the upshot of equal marginal sacrifice is that no dollar should be paid by a poorer person while there are still richer taxpayers available—since a poorer person's tax dollar will always cost that person more in welfare than the loss of a dollar would cost the richer person. Once all remaining incomes are equal, however, each person should pay the same amount of tax.

As dollars are always taken first from those for whom they have less real value, such a tax scheme will also minimize the *total* real sacrifice sustained by all taxpayers. That would have to be the actual point of any such scheme. There is no credible demand of fairness that each person sustain the same real sacrifice from the last dollar paid in tax. The real reason to embrace this approach to taxation is that it minimizes total sacrifice; it is therefore better referred to by its alternative name, the "minimum-sacrifice principle" (Edgeworth 1897, 131).

That taxation should be levied so as to minimize total sacrifice is clearly a utilitarian idea, though not, on the face of it, a very good one, since the utilitarian aim for government, properly expressed, is that of maximizing total welfare. While this might involve arranging taxation so as to ensure minimal overall sacrifice (for a given level of revenue), it also might not, once considerations relating to incentives and other relevant factors are taken into account. The question of the optimal utilitarian tax scheme is not, however, our current concern (we return to it in chapter 6).

32. As we pointed out in note 16, this is equivalent to one interpretation of the benefit principle.

33. Sometimes the principle of proportional sacrifice is defended by pointing out that taxation in proportion to welfare leaves relative levels of welfare unchanged. Thus, two people, with levels of welfare 10 and 100, both taxed so as to reduce their welfare by 10%, end up with levels of welfare 9 and 90, and the 1:10 ratio between their levels of welfare is unchanged. This is said to satisfy some notion of equal treatment or "an identifiable sense of equality" (Witte 1981, 353). Cohen-Stuart had also appealed to this consideration in his defense of proportional sacrifice; see Musgrave (1959), 98, and Edgeworth (1897), 129–30. Of all the odd claims that have been made in the name of tax equity, this is surely one of the very oddest. It is one thing to believe that people either deserve or are entitled to be just as well off, in absolute terms, as the market leaves them, so that we can treat the market-generated distribution of welfare as the proper baseline for consideration of the fair distri-

bution of tax burdens. But it is quite another thing to believe that there is some inherent moral significance to the *relative* levels of welfare found in the market-generated distribution, so that any proportional transformation of that distribution will preserve justice. This is moralization of the market with a vengeance, for it implies that the market is to be praised for yielding an appropriate ranking of persons in terms of relative desert. It seems likely that this defense of the criterion of proportional sacrifice is motivated by a desire to avoid explicitly embracing redistribution for the benefit of the worse off as a requirement of justice.

34. For an excellent survey, including succinct criticism of versions of libertarianism that we ignore here, see Kymlicka (1990), chap. 4.

35. A conclusion explicitly embraced in Nozick (1974), 110–13, 169–72, 265–8.

36. This is the view of Epstein (1985 and 1987).

37. There may also be a problem of vertical equity: the adjustment may sometimes leave an advantage for those in the top bracket, if the bonds have to be priced to find some buyers in lower brackets; see Slemrod and Bakija (2000), 195–6.

38. Auerbach and Hassett (1999), 1; the reference is to Musgrave (1959).

39. See also Kaplow (1989 and forthcoming).

CHAPTER THREE

1. See Locke (1690), chap. 5. For a modern version of the view, see Nozick (1974).

2. See Hume (1739), bk. III, pt. II.

3. For more on the distinction, see Scheffler (1982), and Nagel (1986), chap. 9.

4. See Hegel (1821), secs. 41–53.

5. See Hobbes (1651), chaps. 13 and 14.

6. Many economists continue to adhere to the assumption that interpersonal comparisons of welfare are "meaningless" or at least impossible to make. See, e.g., Slemrod and Bakija (2000), 56. For discussion of this assumption and the limitations it imposes on welfare economics, see Sen (1997), 1–23, 112–4; see also Scanlon (1991). However, it is now also common to waive the ban on interpersonal comparability so that weights for different levels of welfare may be introduced into the social-welfare functions; see, e.g., Atkinson and Stiglitz (1980), 351–2.

Some economists who refuse to allow interpersonal comparisons but recognize the practical uselessness of the Pareto criterion of efficiency embrace the Kaldor-Hicks or "potential compensation" criterion of efficiency, according to which a change is an improvement if the losers could be compensated for their loss by transfers from the winners, the winners remaining better-off after the transfer. For a succinct discussion of these issues as they emerge in the economic analysis of law, see Coleman (1988). For critical discussion of cost-benefit analysis, which attempts to implement the Kaldor-Hicks criterion of efficiency, see Kornhauser (2000).

7. The philosophically most subtle presentation of classical utilitarianism is Sidgwick (1907).

8. See Wiggins (1985).

9. See Rawls (1999b), 19–26.

10. See Parfit (1991).

11. See, especially, Rawls (1999b), chap. 2.

12. For further discussion, see Nagel (1991), chap. 10.

13. See Scanlon (1998), chap. 6.

14. For critical discussion of the related idea that the market rewards people in proportion to what they produce, along with some other claims about the moral significance of market mechanisms, see Sen (1985); for a historical discussion, see Fried (1998), 130–45. See also Gibbard (1985).

15. See Dworkin (2000), chaps. 1 & 2.

16. See chapter 2, section IV.

17. For further discussion of the issues raised in this section, see Nagel (1991), chap. 6.

18. See Murphy (1998).

19. See Cohen (2000).

CHAPTER FOUR

1. For a discussion of these writings, see Musgrave (1959), chap. 4. English translations of some of the originals are found in Musgrave and Peacock (1958). See, especially, Lindahl (1919). Musgrave himself proposes a tripartite division of the functions of government into the Allocation, Distribution, and Stabilization branches, the first two of which are related to our distinction between distribution and public provision.

For more recent discussions, with references to the literature since Musgrave (1959), see Kaplow (1996); Slemrod and Yitzhaki (2001). We find Kaplow's article particularly sympathetic because of his insistence on separating out the redistributive effects of taxation in determining the level of public goods, rather than including them in the cost-benefit calculation by adding in a distributional factor—as is often done.

2. A view of this type is defended in Epstein (1985), 7–18, 283–305; and Epstein (1987).

3. See Samuelson (1954).

4. See Schelling (1984).

5. Such a pure efficiency argument is persuasively stated by E. M. Phelps in his recent defense of wage subsidies; see Phelps (1997).

6. Scanlon (1975).

7. See, e.g., Rawls (1999a); Beitz (1999); Pogge (1992). Economic globalization has made more pressing the question of whether the government of a rich country may adopt policies that are beneficial to poor countries, even if they are detrimental to the interests of poor people in the rich country, who are nevertheless far better off than almost everyone in the poor countries.

CHAPTER FIVE

1. Messere (1998), 3, reports that this idea is no longer seriously in contention in Europe, though it once was.

2. For illuminating discussion of the concepts of income, consumption, and wealth, see Bradford (1986), chap. 2.

3. See Bradford (1986), 313–5. For critical discussion of this claim, see Paul (1997); for a response to Paul, see Bradford (1997). For comprehensive evaluation of the relative simplicity of the flat tax and the current income tax, see Weisbach (2000).

4. On the similarity of the distorting effects on labor supply of consumption and income taxes, see Bradford (1986), 184–5.

5. See Bradford (1986), 179.

6. See Slemrod and Bakija (2000), 184–97.

7. See Slemrod and Bakija (2000), 114–7, 239–41.

8. See Bradford (1986), 189–94.

9. One such proposal, known as the National Retail Sales Tax ("It's Time for a Tea Party in America"), has been prominently supported by Rep. Billy Tauzin (R-LA), Chair of the Energy and Commerce Committee, see www.house.gov/tauzin/cvr.htm (last visited 6/4/2001); another, the "fair tax" ("April 15: Make It Just Another Day"), is sponsored in Congress by Reps. John Linder (R-GA) and Rep. Collin Peterson (D-MN), see www.fairtax.org (last visited 6/4/2001).

10. See Freedom and Fairness Restoration Act of 1995, H.R. 2060 and S. 1050, 104th Cong. (1995) (sponsored by Rep. Armey and Sens. Shelby, Craig, and Helms).

11. The employee bears the burden of the tax on wages in either case; see Slemrod and Bakija (2000), 205.

12. See Hall and Rabushka (1995), 27; see also pp. 25–6, where the authors discuss different definitions of the term "fair" and write that most people understand the term "fair" to mean that "everyone should receive the same, or equal, treatment" (26).

13. See Hall and Rabushka (1996), 28. Indeed, on the first page of Hall and Rabushka (1995), the authors shamelessly help themselves to a notion of fairness incompatible with the one they invoke in their claim that a fair tax "treats everyone the same" (see the previous note): "Our plan is fair to ordinary Americans because it would permit a tax-free allowance of $25,500 for a family of four" (vii).

14. See Bradford (1986), 76–8.

15. See Kotlikoff (1996), 171–2.

16. See Bradford (1988).

17. For discussion, see Zelenak (1999).

18. Kaldor (1993). Rawls expresses some sympathy for Kaldor's proposal, as one part of an overall set of institutions designed to satisfy his two principles of justice; see Rawls (1999b), 246.

19. USA Tax Act of 1995, S. 722, 104th Cong. (1995).

20. As Bradford (1986), 60–4, explains, there could be an income type VAT.

21. See Andrews (1974), 1126; Bradford (1986), 68–9; Graetz (1979), 1602–11.

22. So-called supranormal or windfall returns to investment are taxed by a consumption tax; for a clear account, see Bankman and Fried (1998), 539–46.

23. See Slemrod and Bakija (2000), 112–3.

24. For an extensive investigation of this claim, to which our discussion is indebted, see Fried (1992).

25. Our illustration of the fairness argument follows that in Bankman and Griffith (1992), 380; for an illustration using the cash-flow consumption tax, see Fried (1992), 963–4.

26. See, e.g., Andrews (1974), 1167–9.

27. See Musgrave (1959), 161–3.

28. See Fried (1992), 1012–5.

29. See Bradford (1986), 154–67; see also Andrews (1974), 1167–8.

30. Bradford (1986), 155.

31. See Dworkin (2000). A view of this kind is applied to issues of tax justice by Eric Rakowski; see Rakowski (1991, 1996, and 2000). See Rakowski (2000), 347–57, for perhaps the clearest and most comprehensive statement of the fairness-to-savers argument.

32. We leave aside an important complexity in Dworkin's and similar views concerning different kinds of luck and the role of insurance in converting "brute luck," which can disturb the justice of a distribution of holdings, into "option luck," which does not; see Dworkin (2000), chap. 2.

33. For further discussion, see Fleurbaey (1995); Murphy (1996); Hurley (forthcoming).

34. See Bradford (1986), 156.

35. Bradford embraces a progressive consumption tax in recognition that people do not, in fact, have equal starting places. See Bradford (1980), 108.

36. For Dworkin's account of the role of taxation in securing justice, see Dworkin (2000), chap. 2.

37. Fried (1992), 999.

38. See Fried (1992), 1007–8; Bankman and Griffith (1992), 382.

39. Kaldor (1993), 53.

40. The clearest endorsement of the argument is from Charles Fried (Fried 1978, 147–50); see also Andrews (1974), 1166. Stiglitz (2000) cites this as "one of the most forceful arguments against income as a fair basis of taxation" (470). It is mildly endorsed as a "commonsense precept of justice" by Rawls (Rawls 1999b, 246).

41. See Warren (1980), 1094–5.

42. Kaldor (1993), 53.

43. Smith (1789), bk. II, ch. III.

44. Hobbes (1651), chap. 30.

45. On the different rates of saving, see Hubbard, Skinner, and Zeldes (1995), 364-72.

46. Bradford (1986), 162.

47. See, e.g., Musgrave (1996), 733–4. Even Andrews, one of the most influential supporters of a cash-flow consumption tax, writes: "It may well be unacceptable to rely solely on consumption as a personal tax base because for some people wealth has a welfare value above and beyond the deferred consumption it may operate to support, and a consumption tax will reach consumption only in its tangible forms. This is the strongest argument against sole reliance on a personal consumption tax" (Andrews 1975, 956).

48. See Simons (1938), 97.

49. See Schenk (2000), 463–4, and references given there. The Meade Committee Report cites "security, independence, influence and power," see Institute for Fiscal Studies (1978), 351.

50. See *The Politics*, bk. IV, ch. ix; see also Rawls (1999b), 245–6.

51. See Veblen (1899).

52. See Frank (1999 and 2000).

53. For very helpful overviews of the issues mentioned in this and the following paragraph, with extensive references to the economics literature, see Bankman and Fried (1998), and Fried (1999b).

54. See Kotlikoff (1989), 79–80; see also Fried (1999b), 651n.24 and references given there.

55. See Fried (1999b), 642. For a comprehensive discussion by one of the main protagonists in the debate, see Kotlikoff (1989).

56. See Kaplow and Shavell (1994).

57. See Shakow and Shuldiner (2000); Schenk (2000); Bankman (2000).

58. See Fried (2000), which is a comment on the justice-based argument against wealth taxation in Rakowski (2000).

59. See Bankman and Griffith (1992); Bankman and Fried (1998); Cunningham (1996). Human capital and supernormal returns to financial capital are taxed under both an income and a consumption tax; see Bankman and Fried (1998), 539–46.

60. See Cunningham (1996), 21.

61. See, e.g., Bradford (1997), 224–5.

62. Bankman and Griffith (1992), 392–3.

63. The extent and exact nature of the problem depends on the extent to which investment losses are deductible and investors can make the required portfolio adjustments without significant cost. For discussion, see Bankman and Griffith (1992), 397–403.

64. See Schenk (2000), 473.

65. For a compelling defense of the idea that the marginal value of wealth declines more slowly than that of consumption, see Carroll (2000).

66. As does the "left" or "real" libertarianism of Philippe Van Parijs, according to which a just society ensures that "each person has the greatest possible opportunity to do whatever she might want to do" (Van Parijs 1995, 25). A similar view is found in Ackerman and Alstott (1999).

67. Daniel Shaviro argues that there is an additional reason why theorists concerned with welfare should prefer the endowment base: the higher the potential income people have (the higher their "wage rate"), the better off they are. For example, take two people, Andrea and Brian, where Andrea's potential income is higher, but actual income lower (though leisure time greater), than Brian's. Andrea is better off than Brian, since she *could* have just as much leisure as Brian with more income but prefers the life she has. See Shaviro (2000a), 402–6. This claim requires the assumption that both people derive the same utility from each possible income-earning option and differ only in their taste for leisure (p. 404). But it is

clear that some people's preferences over possible jobs—taking into account not only the wage but also how much they would value the job for its own sake—are better served by the market than others. Andrea might hate all the high-paying jobs. See also Murphy (1996), 482–4.

68. See, e.g., Kelman (1979), 842; Rakowski (2000), 267n.10.

69. On different conceptions of liberty and autonomy, see chapter 3, section X. For discussion of positive legal duties, see Murphy (2001).

70. See Nozick (1974), 169–71.

71. See Nozick (1974), 169.

72. On this last point, see Shaviro (2000a), 414.

73. See Shaviro (2000a), 410.

74. See Shaviro (2000a), 412, 415–6.

75. Several European countries tax the imputed rent on owner-occupied housing; see Messere (1993), 234.

76. This departs somewhat from legal usage; see Chirelstein (1999), 1–2.

77. It must be remembered that, as with the case of wealth, the question for such theories is not, Would these exclusions have a place in a tax code designed for a world that already exhibits the relevant kind equality of opportunity?—but rather, Would these exclusions have a place in a tax code part of the aim of which is to bring about equality of opportunity? Therefore, it cannot simply be assumed that, say, the favorable tax treatment of owner-occupied housing interferes with equality of opportunity.

78. See, e.g., Bradford (1986), 161.

79. See Messere (1998), 11.

80. For excellent and succinct discussions of the current tax treatment of housing, see Chirelstein (1999), 175-8; Slemrod and Bakija (2000), 185–90.

81. See Auten, Clotfelter, and Schmalbeck (2000), 403–14.

82. Though for some this may be the whole point: "Simply, an argument may be made that some institutions are richer contributors to the social, cultural, and intellectual mosaic than others. Hence, it may be possible to justify a system of deduction that is skewed in the direction of the favourite charities of upper-income taxpayers" (Woodman 1988, 575).

For an early critique of the charitable deduction, see McDaniel (1972). For the Canadian experience with a two-tier credit (17% of the first $200 donated and 29% of amounts over $200) for charitable contributions, see Duff (2001).

83. See Feldstein (1976). Even the first income tax scheme should

be understood as a piece of reform, in the relevant sense, since it changed the ground rules of economic life.

84. See Slemrod and Bakija (2000), 177–180.

85. For a book-length treatment of this issue from a utilitarian perspective, see Shaviro (2000b).

86. See chapter 3, section IX.

CHAPTER SIX

1. The Economic Growth and Tax Relief Reconciliation Act of 2001 reduces all marginal rates and introduces a new 10% bracket. However, the act expires at the end of 2010, so unless Congress takes further steps, the highest marginal rate in 2011 will once more be 39.6%. For detailed accounts of this bizarre piece of legislation, see Joint Committee on Taxation (2001) and Manning and Windish (2001).

2. See Chirelstein (1999), 3–4, 182. And there's more: the 39.6% rate was enacted as a 36% rate with a 10% surcharge.

3. H.R. 1040 (1999).

4. See http://flattax.house.gov/proposal/flat-sum.asp (last visited June 6, 2001).

5. On the rise of this kind of misleading rhetoric in the 1990s in the U.S. Congress, see Kornhauser (1996b).

6. For discussion of this common rhetorical ploy, see Fried (1999a).

7. See, generally, Slemrod and Bakija (2000), 64–75.

8. See Bradford (1995).

9. Blum and Kalven (1952), 487. The quote is from Simons (1938), 18. For further criticism of Blum and Kalven's approach, which proceeds on the assumption that proportional taxation requires no defense but progressive taxation does, see Fried (1999a).

10. See, generally, Sen (1997).

11. See chapter 3, section VI.

12. See Parfit (1991), and Temkin (1993).

13. Rawls (1999b), 64.

14. Rawls (1999b), 64. The issue of how equality-of-opportunity theories should assess social outcomes has generated a variety of proposals from philosophers. For example, Ronald Dworkin has made a suggestion turning on the idea of a hypothetical insurance market for abilities. See Dworkin (2000), 83–109. For a different proposal and an overview of the issues raised here, see Rakowski (1991), chap. 6. For Van Parijs's approach, see Van Parijs (1995), chap. 3.

15. For accessible and very helpful critical discussion, see Slemrod and Bakija (2000), 103–132; Slemrod (1990); Slemrod (1998).

16. See, e.g., Bankman and Griffith (1987); Slemrod (1990).

17. For overviews of the effects of varying different assumptions, see Slemrod and Bakija (forthcoming); Zelenak and Moreland (1999). As Slemrod notes, a particularly contestable assumption of most models is that "the rich are different from the poor in only one way: they are endowed with the ability to command a higher market wage, which is presumed to reflect a higher real productivity of their labor effort" (Slemrod 2000, 12). This ignores the role of luck, tastes, inheritance, among other possibilities; see pp. 12–13.

18. Slemrod and Bakija (2000), 107. See also Slemrod (1998) and (2000), 3–28; Moffitt and Wilhelm (2000).

19. See Feldstein (1995 and 1997).

20. See Auten and Carroll (1999); Goolsbee (2000); Gruber and Saez (2000). The technical magnitude economists use to capture the significance of this effect is that of the elasticity of taxable income with respect to the after-tax return—the percentage change in taxable income that results from a 1% change in the after-tax return. While Feldstein reached estimates of this elasticity ranging from 1 to 3, more recent estimates tend to be significantly less, around 0.5.

21. See Gruber and Saez (2000), Table 10, the case of the "Utilitarian: Progressive" criterion. Because of the demogrant, the scheme remains progressive.

22. See Slemrod (1998), 780–1.

23. See Slemrod (1998), 778–9; Slemrod and Kopczuk (forthcoming).

24. So much so that Zelenak and Moreland (1999) are moved to design an optimal tax model without a demogrant; the result turns out to be the rehabilitation of graduated rates.

25. Stiglitz (2000), 562; see also Slemrod (1990), 166–8; and the opening paragraphs of Gruber and Saez (2000).

26. See Hershkoff and Loffredo (1997); Slemrod and Bakija (forthcoming).

27. See Bernstein et al. (2000); Wolff (1996 and 2000).

28. See Simons (1938), 17.

29. By the Economic Growth and Tax Relief Reconciliation Act of 2001; see Joint Committee on Taxation (2001) and Manning and Windish (2001). Citizens for Tax Justice estimate that the richest 1% of taxpayers, those with annual incomes of $373,000 or more, will receive 25.1% of the income tax cuts introduced by this act and 37.6% of the combined cuts to the income and estate taxes. See http://www.ctj.org/html/gwbfinal.htm (last visited July 5, 2001).

CHAPTER SEVEN

1. Wolff (2000).

2. See chapter 5, section VI.

3. See Pechman (1987), 235–6; Davenport and Soled (1999), 593.

4. On the trend in inequality of wealth, see Wolff (1996 and 2000).

5. See Joint Committee on Taxation (2001), and Manning and Windish (2001).

6. Presidential Debate, Washington University, St Louis, October 17, 2000. Transcript available at http://www.debates.org/transcripts/ (last visited June 7, 2001).

7. Including some tax policy theorists: Hall and Rabushka (1995), 126, write that an "inheritance tax constitutes double taxation, which violates a sacred principle of sound tax policy." "Sacred" seems a bit strong.

8. "Although it is hard to deny the symbolic power of numerology throughout cultural history, it seems out of place in discussing tax system design. The no-economic-double-tax principle cannot be a fairness norm. Fairness has to do with the relative tax burdens among people, not things" (Dodge 1996, 563, footnote omitted).

9. See Davenport and Soled (1999), 594–5.

10. See Poterba (2000), 330–1; Gale and Slemrod (2001), sec. 1. Once the tax begins to bite, it is charged to the donor or the donor's estate at a rate starting at 37% and going up to 55%; a surcharge on estates over $10 million raises the rate to 60% until it phases out the benefit of marginal rates less than 55%. For the changes introduced by the 2001 legislation, see Manning and Windish (2001).

11. See Pechman (1987), 240–9; Poterba (2000), 341–5.

12. See Graetz (1983), 270–3.

13. See, generally, Holtz-Eakin (1996); Repetti (2000).

14. See chapter 5, sections III & IV.

15. However, the 2001 legislation provides that from 2010, after the abolition of the estate tax, the amount by which each estate is permitted to increase the basis of its appreciated assets will be limited to $1.3 million; see Manning and Windish (2001).

16. Though typically the argument is made by appeal to the *concepts* of income or consumption. See, e.g., Simons (1938), 56–8, 125–47; Canada. Royal Commission on Taxation (1966), 3: 465–519. Institute for Fiscal Studies (1978), 40–2, 137, 183-5.

17. Among OECD countries, inheritance taxes, levied on donees, are now far more common than estate taxes levied on donors; see Messere (1993), 302–5.

18. See Bradford (1986), 37–8.

19. See Dodge (1978), 1187. See also Bradford (1986), 97n.d., who cites the difficulty of measuring accruing wealth from anticipated inheritance.

20. See Fried (1999b) and references given there.

21. See Carnegie (1962), 19–21.

22. See Dodge (1978 and 1996); Ascher (1990).

23. For the claim about accuracy, see Slemrod (2000), 5.

24. See Dodge (1978), 1181.

25. See Dodge (1996), 574; for helpful discussion of the situation of business heirs under the estate tax, see Davenport and Soled (1999), 609–18; Gale and Slemrod (2001).

26. This is one of the main bases for Edward McCaffery's supposedly "liberal" case for the abolition of the estate tax; see McCaffery (1994a and 1994b). For effective criticism of McCaffrey's argument, see Alstott (1996b) and Rakowski (1996).

27. See Rosen (1995), 497; Gale and Perozek (2001).

28. See, e.g., Alstott (1996b), 385–6.

29. See, e.g., Holtz-Eakin (1996), 512-4; Holtz-Eakin is here discussing the behavioral consequences of the estate tax, but the conclusion applies to the behavioral consequences of any reduction in the post-tax value of a gift or bequest. See also Rosen (1995), 498.

30. See Holtz-Eakin (1996), 513.

31. Kaplow (1995b).

32. See Fried (1999b), 670–1.

33. Dodge (1996), 576.

34. For a general critical discussion of this assumption, see Sen (1977).

35. See Dodge (1996), 570–1, for a discussion of this kind; Dodge attributes the idea to Daniel Shaviro.

36. Short of interfering with the principle of testamentary (not to mention donative) freedom; see Dodge (1996), 530–1.

37. Institute for Fiscal Studies (1978), 318.

38. For a clear statement to this effect, see Rakowski (1996).

39. See Rakowski (1991), 158–66.

40. For detailed discussion, see Sandford, Willis, and Ironside (1973); Halbach (1988).

41. See Institute for Fiscal Studies (1978), 320.

42. See Rakowski (2000), 334–47.

43. If unrealized gains were taxed at death and gratuitous receipts included in the donee's tax base, the revenue from abolishing the estate tax would be more than made up. See Galvin (1999), 1326; see also Galvin (1991).

44. See chapter 3, sections VIII and IX.

45. See Becker (1993).

46. See Nagel (1991), chap. 10.

47. See Ascher (1990), 91.

48. I.R.C. § 1014 provides for the step-up in basis. See note 15 for amendments to this provision scheduled to take effect in 2010.

49. For discussion, see Zelenak (1993), which plausibly argues that taxation of capital gains at death—in effect treating death as a realization event—is preferable to carrying over the decedent's basis in the event of a realization by the donee. See also Dodge (1994).

50. In addition, it would open up significant opportunities for avoidance of federal and state income tax. See Blattmachr and Gans (2001).

51. Wicksell (1896), 111.

CHAPTER EIGHT

1. In some countries, including Germany and Italy, the idea of horizontal equity has been elevated to the level of constitutional principle; see Vanistendael (1996), 20-3.

2. See McDaniel and Surrey (1985).

3. In *Moritz v. Commissioner*, 469 F2d 466 (10th Cir 1972), the court ruled that a former provision of the I.R.C., which allowed a deduction for dependent-care expenses for women, but not men, who had never married, was unconstitutional. "We conclude that the classification is an invidious discrimination and invalid under due process principles. . . . The statute did not make the challenged distinction as part of a scheme dealing with the varying burdens of dependents' care borne by taxpayers, but instead made a special discrimination premised on sex alone, which cannot stand" (469 F2d 466, 470).

4. An early exploration of sex discrimination through taxation is Blumberg (1972); see further section III. In recent years there has been more focus on issues of tax discrimination on the basis of sex, race, and sexual orientation. See Alstott (1996a); Brown and Fellows (1996); Cain (1991); McCaffery (1997); Moran and Whitford (1996).

5. In Italy, joint taxation of married couples has been held to violate constitutional principles of equality and taxation in accordance with ability to pay; see Vanistendael (1996), 22-3. In Germany, a marriage penalty was held to violate a constitutional provision requiring the special protection of marriage and the family by the state; see Vanistendael (1996), 28.

6. Reported in *The New York Times*, Feb. 11, 2000, p. A22.

7. See Bittker (1975). That article also makes the point about standard of living described below.

8. Quite apart from the difference that follows from the single individual's having one personal exemption and the couple's having two.

9. This basic structure is not disturbed by the "Marriage Penalty Relief" provisions of the 2001 tax legislation. Despite the label, those provisions actually benefit all married taxpayers, whether they receive a penalty or a bonus. See Joint Committee on Taxation (2001); Manning and Windish (2001).

10. There is also a marriage penalty for the Earned Income Tax Credit, which we leave aside. It is alleviated somewhat by the 2001 tax legislation; see Joint Committee on Taxation (2001); Manning and Windish (2001).

11. See chapter 2, section VIII.

12. Clear evidence of the sensitivity of employment decisions by married women to differences in the marginal tax rate is presented in Eissa (1995). There is, however, some debate about the magnitude and precise nature of this behavioral effect; for discussion, with references, see Alstott (1996a), 2017–22.

13. For defense of compulsory separate filing, see Kornhauser (1993); Zelenak (1994). For the argument that the current scheme discriminates against women, see Blumberg (1972), and McCaffery (1997).

CHAPTER NINE

1. For an empirical study indicating the importance of sentiments of fairness in people's evaluation of tax reform, see Hite and Roberts (1992).

2. A heartening example is the recent defense of the estate tax by a group of tycoons headed by Warren Buffett and William Gates, Sr.

3. See Nagel (1991), and Murphy (2001).

4. For illuminating discussion of the options, see Shaviro (1997).

5. A detailed proposal is presented in Phelps (1997).

6. It phases out at a rate of 21.06% of income above $11,610. See I.R.C. sec. 32.

7. See references given in chapter 6, n. 18.

8. See reference given in chapter 5, n. 23.

9. See references given in chapter 6, n. 23.

10. See Carroll, Holtz-Eakin, Rider, and Rosen (2000). The authors note that "entrepreneurial enterprises account for at least 10 percent of the economy's nonresidential fixed investment" (427).

References

Ackerman, Bruce and Anne Alstott. 1999. *The Stakeholder Society.* New Haven and London: Yale University Press.

Alstott, Anne L. 1996a. Tax Policy and Feminism: Competing Goals and Institutional Choices. *Columbia Law Review* 96: 2001–82.

———. 1996b. The Uneasy Liberal Case Against Income and Wealth Transfer Taxation. *Tax Law Review* 51: 363–402.

Andrews, William. 1974. A Consumption-Type or Cash Flow Personal Income Tax. *Harvard Law Review* 87: 1113–88.

———. 1975. Fairness and the Personal Income Tax: A Reply to Professor Warren. *Harvard Law Review* 88: 947–58.

Aristotle. *The Politics.*

Ascher, Mark L. 1990. Curtailing Inherited Wealth. *Michigan Law Review* 89: 69–151.

Atkinson, Anthony B. and Joseph E. Stiglitz. 1980. *Lectures on Public Economics.* New York: McGraw-Hill.

Auerbach, Alan J. and Kevin A. Hassett. 1999. A New Measure of Horizontal Equity. NBER Working Paper No. 7035.

Auten, Gerald and Robert Carroll. 1999. The Effect of Income Taxes on Household Income. *The Review of Economics and Statistics* 81: 681–93.

Auten, Gerald, Charles T. Clotfelter, and Richard L. Schmalbeck. 2000. Taxes and Philanthropy Among the Wealthy. In Slemrod (2000), 392–424.

Bankman, Joseph. 2000. What Can We Say About a Wealth Tax? *Tax Law Review* 53: 477–87.

Bankman, Joseph and Barbara H. Fried. 1998. Winners and Losers in the Shift to A Consumption Tax. *Georgetown Law Journal* 86: 539–68.

Bankman, Joseph and Thomas Griffith. 1987. Social Welfare and the Rate Structure: A New Look at Progressive Taxation. *California Law Review* 75: 1905–67.

———. 1992. Is the Debate Between an Income Tax and a Consumption Tax a Debate about Risk? Does it Matter? *Tax Law Review* 47: 377–406.

Becker, Gary S. 1993. *Human Capital*. 3rd ed. Chicago: University of Chicago Press.

Beitz, Charles. 1999. *Political Theory and International Relations*. Rev. ed. Princeton: Princeton University Press.

Bernstein, Jared, Elizabeth C. McNichol, Lawrence Mishel, and Robert Zahradnik. 2000. *Pulling Apart: A State-by-State Analysis of Income Trends*. Washington, D.C.: Center on Budget and Policy Priorities and Economic Policy Institute.

Bittker, Boris I. 1975. Federal Income Taxation and the Family. *Stanford Law Review* 27: 1389–1463.

Blattmachr, Jonathan G. and Mitchell M. Gans. 2001. Wealth Transfer Tax Repeal: Some Thoughts on Policy and Planning. *Tax Notes* 90: 393–99

Blum, Walter J. and Harry Kalven, Jr. 1952. The Uneasy Case for Progressive Taxation. *University of Chicago Law Review* 19: 417–520.

Blumberg, Grace. 1972. Sexism in the Code: A Comparative Study of Income Taxation of Working Wives and Mothers. *Buffalo Law Review* 21: 49–98.

Boskin, Michael J., ed. 1996. *Frontiers of Tax Reform*. Stanford, Calif.: Hoover Institution Press.

Bradford, David F. 1980. The Case for a Personal Consumption Tax. In *What Should Be Taxed: Income or Consumption?*, ed. Joseph A. Pechman, 75–125. Washington, D.C.: Brookings Institution Press.

———. 1986. *Untangling the Income Tax*. Cambridge, Mass.: Harvard University Press.

———. 1988. What Are Consumption Taxes and Who Pays Them? *Tax Notes* 39: 383–91.

———, ed. 1995. *Distributional Analysis of Tax Policy*. Washington, D.C.: AEI Press.

———. 1997. What's in a Name? Income, Consumption, and the

Sources of Tax Complexity. *North Carolina Law Review* 76: 223–31.

Brown, Karen B. and Mary Louise Fellows, eds. 1996. *Taxing America.* New York and London: New York University Press.

Cain, Patricia A. 1991. Same-Sex Couples and the Federal Tax Laws. *Law & Sexuality* 1: 97–131.

Canada. Royal Commission on Taxation. 1966. Report of the Royal Commission on Taxation. 7 vols. Ottawa: Queen's Printer.

Carnegie, Andrew. [1900] 1962. *The Gospel of Wealth.* Cambridge, Mass.: Harvard University Press.

Carroll, Christopher D. 2000. "Why Do the Rich Save So Much?" In Slemrod (2000), 465–84.

Carroll, Robert, Douglas Holtz-Eakin, Mark Rider, and Harvey S. Rosen. 2000. Entrepreneurs, Income Taxes, and Investment. In Slemrod (2000), 427–55.

Chirelstein, Marvin. 1999. *Federal Income Taxation.* Rev. 8th ed. New York: Foundation Press.

Cohen, G. A. 2000. *If You're an Egalitarian, How Come You're So Rich?* Cambridge, Mass.: Harvard University Press.

Coleman, Jules L. 1988. Efficiency, Utility, and Wealth Maximization. In Coleman, *Markets, Morals and the Law*, 95–132. New York: Cambridge University Press.

Cunningham, Noel B. 1996. The Taxation of Capital Income and the Choice of Tax Base. *Tax Law Review* 52: 17–44.

Davenport, Charles and Jay A. Soled. 1999. Enlivening the Death-Tax Death-Talk. *Tax Notes* 84: 591–631.

Dodge, Joseph M. 1978. Beyond Estate and Gift Tax Reform: Including Gifts and Bequests in Income. *Harvard Law Review* 91: 1177–1211.

———. 1994. Further Thoughts on Realizing Gains and Losses at Death. *Vanderbilt Law Review* 47: 1827–61.

———. 1996. Taxing Gratuitous Transfers Under a Consumption Tax. *Tax Law Review* 51: 529–99.

Duff, David G. 2001. Charitable Contributions and the Personal Income Tax: Evaluating the Canadian Credit. In *Between State and Market*, ed. Jim Phillips, Bruce Chapman, and David Stevens, 407–56. Montreal and Kingston: McGill-Queens University Press.

Dworkin, Ronald. 2000. *Sovereign Virtue.* Cambridge, Mass.: Harvard University Press.

Edgeworth, F. Y. 1897. The Pure Theory of Taxation. Reprinted in Musgrave and Peacock (1958), 119–36.

Eissa, Nada. 1995. Taxation and Labor Supply of Married Women:

The Tax Reform Act of 1986 as a Natural Experiment. NBER Working Paper No. 5023.

Epstein, Richard. 1985. *Takings*. Cambridge, Mass.: Harvard University Press.

———. 1987. Taxation in a Lockean World. In *Philosophy and Law*, ed. Jules Coleman and Ellen Frankel Paul, 49–74. Oxford and New York: Basil Blackwell.

Feldstein, Martin. 1976. On the Theory of Tax Reform. *Journal of Public Economics* 6: 77–104.

———. 1995. The Effect of Marginal Tax Rates on Taxable Income. *Journal of Political Economy* 103: 551–72.

———. 1997. How Big Should Government Be? *National Tax Journal* 50: 197–213.

Fleurbaey, Marc. 1995. Equal Opportunity or Equal Social Outcome? *Economics & Philosophy* 11: 25–55.

Frank, Robert H. 1999. *Luxury Fever*. New York: Free Press.

———. 2000. Progressive Taxation and the Incentive Problem. In Slemrod (2000), 490–507.

Fried, Barbara H. 1992. Fairness and the Consumption Tax. *Stanford Law Review* 44: 961–1017.

———. 1998. *The Progressive Assault on Laissez Faire*. Cambridge, Mass.: Harvard University Press.

———. 1999a. The Puzzling Case for Proportionate Taxation. *Chapman Law Review* 2: 157–95.

———. 1999b. Who Gets Utility from Bequests? The Distributive and Welfare Implications for a Consumption Tax. *Stanford Law Review* 51: 641–81.

———. 2000. Compared to What? Taxing Brute Luck and Other Second-Best Problems. *Tax Law Review* 53: 377–95.

Fried, Charles. 1978. *Right and Wrong*. Cambridge, Mass.: Harvard University Press.

Gale, William G., James R. Hines Jr., and Joel Slemrod, eds. 2001. *Rethinking Estate and Gift Taxation*. Washington, D.C.: Brookings Institution Press.

Gale, William G. and Maria G. Perozek. 2001. Do Estate Taxes Reduce Saving? In Gale, Hines, and Slemrod (2001), 216–57.

Gale, William G. and Joel Slemrod. 2001. Overview. In Gale, Hines, and Slemrod (2001), 1–64.

Galvin, Charles O. 1991. To Bury the Estate Tax, Not to Praise It. *Tax Notes* 52: 1413–19.

———. 1999. Death-Tax, Death-Talk, A Reply. *Tax Notes* 84: 1325–6.

Gibbard, Allan. 1985. What's Morally Special About Free Exchange? *Social Philosophy and Policy* 2: 20–28.

————. 1991. Constructing Justice. *Philosophy & Public Affairs* 20: 264–79.

Goolsbee, Austan. 2000. What Happens When You Tax the Rich? *Journal of Political Economy* 108: 352–78.

Gordon, David M. 1972. Taxation of the Poor and the Normative Theory of Tax Incidence. *American Economic Review* 62: 319–28.

Graetz, Michael J. 1979. Implementing a Progressive Consumption Tax. *Harvard Law Review* 92: 1575–1657.

————. 1983. To Praise the Estate Tax, Not to Bury It. *Yale Law Journal* 93: 259–86.

————. 1995. Distributional Tables, Tax Legislation, and the Illusion of Precision. In Bradford (1995), 15–78.

Griffith, Thomas. 1993. Should "Tax Norms" Be Abandoned? Rethinking Tax Policy Analysis and the Taxation of Personal Injury Recoveries. *Wisconsin Law Review* 1993: 1115–61.

Gruber, Jon and Emmanuel Saez. 2000. The Elasticity of Taxable Income: Evidence and Implications. NBER Working Paper No. 7512.

Halbach, Edward C., Jr. 1988. An Accessions Tax. *Real Property, Probate and Trust Journal* 23: 211–74.

Hall, Robert E. and Alvin Rabushka. 1995. *The Flat Tax*. 2nd ed. Stanford, Calif.: Hoover Institution Press.

————. 1996. The Flat Tax: A Simple, Progressive Consumption Tax. In Boskin (1996), 27–53.

Hart, H. L. A. 1994. *The Concept of Law*. 2nd ed. Oxford: Clarendon Press.

Hassett Kevin A., and R. Glenn Hubbard, eds. Forthcoming. *Inequality and Tax Policy*. Washington, D.C.: AEI Press.

Hayek, F. A. 1960. *The Constitution of Liberty*. Chicago: University of Chicago Press.

Hegel, G. W. F. 1821. *The Philosophy of Right*.

Hershkoff, Helen and Stephen Loffredo. 1997. *The Rights of the Poor*. Carbondale and Edwardsville: Southern Illinois Univ. Press.

Hite, Peggy A. and Michael L. Roberts. 1992. An Analysis of Tax Reform Based on Taxpayers' Perceptions of Fairness and Self-Interest. In *Advances in Taxation*, vol. 4, ed. Jerrold J. Stern, 115–37. Greenwich, Ct.: JAI Press.

Hobbes, Thomas. 1651. *Leviathan*.

Holtz-Eakin, Douglas. 1996. The Uneasy Empirical Case for Abolishing the Estate Tax. *Tax Law Review* 51: 495–515.

Hubbard, R. Glenn, Jonathan Skinner, and Stephen P. Zeldes. 1995. Precautionary Saving and Social Insurance. *Journal of Political Economy* 73: 360–99.

Hume, David. 1739. *A Treatise of Human Nature.*

Hurley, S. L. Forthcoming. *Justice, Luck, and Knowledge.* Cambridge, Mass. and London: Harvard University Press.

Institute for Fiscal Studies. 1978. *The Structure and Reform of Direct Taxation* (The Meade Committee Report). London: Allen & Unwin.

Joint Committee on Taxation. 1993. *Methodology and Issues in Measuring Changes in the Distribution of Tax Burdens.* Washington, D.C.: Superintendent of Documents, JCS-7–93.

———. 2001. *Summary of Provisions Contained in the Conference Agreement for H.R. 1836, the Economic Growth and Tax Relief Reconciliation Act of 2001.* Washington, D.C.: Superintendent of Documents, JCX-50–01.

Kaldor, Nicholas. [1955] 1993. *An Expenditure Tax.* Aldershot: Gregg Revivals.

Kaplow, Louis. 1989. Horizontal Equity: Measures in Search of a Principle. *National Tax Journal* 42: 139–54.

———. 1995a. A Fundamental Objection to Tax Equity Norms: A Call for Utilitarianism. *National Tax Journal* 48: 497–514.

———. 1995b. A Note on Subsidizing Gifts. *Journal of Public Economics* 58: 469–77.

———. 1996. The Optimal Supply of Public Goods and the Distortionary Cost of Taxation. *National Tax Journal* 49: 513–33.

———. Forthcoming. Horizontal Equity: New Measures, Unclear Principles. In Hassett and Hubbard (forthcoming).

Kaplow, Louis and Stephen Shavell. 1994. Why the Legal System is Less Efficient than the Income Tax in Redistributing Income. *Journal of Legal Studies* 23: 667–81.

———. 2001. Fairness versus Welfare. *Harvard Law Review* 114: 961–1388.

Kelman, Mark G. 1979. Personal Deductions Revisited. *Stanford Law Review* 31: 831–83.

Kiesling, Herbert. 1992. *Taxation and Public Goods.* Ann Arbor: University of Michigan Press.

Kornhauser, Lewis. 2000. On Justifying Cost-Benefit Analysis. *Journal of Legal Studies* 29: 1037–57.

Kornhauser, Marjorie E. 1993. Love, Money, and the IRS. *Hastings Law Journal* 45: 63–111.

———. 1996a. Equality, Liberty, and a Fair Income Tax. *Fordham Urban Law Journal* 23: 607–61.

———. 1996b. The Rise of Rhetoric in Tax Reform Debate: An Example. *Tulane Law Review* 70: 2345–71.

Kotlikoff, Laurence J. 1989. *What Determines Savings?* Cambridge, Mass. and London: MIT Press.

———. 1996. Saving and Consumption Taxation: The Federal Retail Sales Tax Example. In Boskin (1996), 160–80.

Kymlicka, Will. 1990. *Contemporary Political Philosophy*. Oxford: Clarendon Press.

Lindahl, Erik. 1919. Just Taxation—a Positive Solution. In Musgrave and Peacock (1958).

Locke, John. 1690. *Second Treatise of Government*.

McCaffery, Edward J. 1994a. The Political Liberal Case Against the Estate Tax. *Philosophy & Public Affairs* 23: 281–312.

———. 1994b. The Uneasy Case for Wealth Transfer Taxation. *Yale Law Journal* 104: 283–365.

———. 1997. *Taxing Women*. Chicago and London: University of Chicago Press.

McDaniel, Paul R. 1972. Federal Matching Grants for Charitable Deductions: A Substitute for the Income Tax Deduction. *Tax Law Review* 27: 377–413.

McDaniel, Paul R. and Stanley S. Surrey. 1985. *Tax Expenditures*. Cambridge, Mass.: Harvard University Press.

Manning, Robert F. and David F. Windish. 2001. Tax Analysts' Guide to the Economic Growth and Tax Relief Reconciliation Act of 2001. *Tax Notes* 91: 1773–1811.

Messere, Ken C. 1993. *Tax Policy in OECD Countries*. Amsterdam: IBFD Publications.

———. 1998. *The Tax System in Industrialized Countries*. Oxford: Oxford University Press.

Mill, John Stuart. 1871. *Principles of Political Economy*.

Mirrlees, J. A. 1971. An Exploration in the Theory of Optimum Income Taxation. *Review of Economic Studies* 38: 175–208.

———. 1986. The Theory of Optimal Taxation. In *Handbook of Mathematical Economics*, vol. 3, ed. Kenneth J. Arrow and Michael D. Intriligator, 1197–1249. Amsterdam: North-Holland.

Moffitt, Robert A. and Mark O. Wilhelm. 2000. Taxation and the Labor Supply Decisions of the Affluent. In Slemrod (2000), 193–234.

Moran, Beverly I. and William Whitford. 1996. A Black Critique of the Internal Revenue Code. *Wisconsin Law Review* 1996: 751–820.

Murphy, Liam. 1996. Liberty, Equality, Well-Being: Rakowski on Wealth Transfer Taxation. *Tax Law Review* 51: 473–94.

———. 1998. Institutions and the Demands of Justice. *Philosophy & Public Affairs* 27: 251–91.

———. 2000. *Moral Demands in Nonideal Theory*. New York: Oxford University Press.

———. 2001. Beneficence, Law, and Liberty. *Georgetown Law Journal* 89: 605–65.

Musgrave, Richard A. 1959. *The Theory of Public Finance*. New York: McGraw-Hill.

———. 1996. Clarifying Tax Reform. *Tax Notes* 70: 731–6.

Musgrave, Richard A. and Peggy B. Musgrave. 1989. *Public Finance in Theory and Practice*. 5th ed. New York: McGraw-Hill.

Musgrave, Richard A. and Alan T. Peacock, eds. 1958. *Classics in the Theory of Public Finance*. London and New York: Macmillan.

Nagel, Thomas. 1986. *The View From Nowhere*. New York: Oxford University Press.

———. 1991. *Equality and Partiality*. New York: Oxford University Press.

Nozick, Robert. 1974. *Anarchy, State, and Utopia*. New York: Basic Books.

Parfit, Derek. 1991. Equality or Priority? The Lindley Lecture. Lawrence: University of Kansas.

Paul, Deborah L. 1997. The Sources of Tax Complexity: How Much Simplicity Can Fundamental Tax Reform Achieve? *North Carolina Law Review* 76: 151–221.

Pechman, Joseph A. 1987. *Federal Tax Policy*. 5th ed. Washington, D.C.: Brookings Institution Press.

Phelps, E. M. 1997. *Rewarding Work*. Cambridge, Mass.: Harvard University Press.

Pigou, A. C. 1947. *A Study in Public Finance*. 3rd ed. London: Macmillan.

Pogge, Thomas. 1992. Cosmopolitanism and Sovereignty. *Ethics* 103: 48–75.

Poterba, James M. 2000. The Estate Tax and After-Tax Investment Returns. In Slemrod (2000), 329–49.

Rakowski, Eric. 1991. *Equal Justice*. Oxford: Clarendon Press.

———. 1996. Transferring Wealth Liberally. *Tax Law Review* 51: 419–72.

———. 2000. Can Wealth Taxes Be Justified? *Tax Law Review* 53: 263–376.

Rawls, John. 1999a. *The Law of Peoples*. Cambridge, Mass. And London: Harvard University Press.

———. 1999b. *A Theory of Justice*. Revised ed. Cambridge, Mass.: Harvard University Press.

Repetti, James R. 2000. The Case for the Estate and Gift Tax. *Tax Notes* 86: 1493–1510.

Rosen, Harvey S. 1995. *Public Finance*. 4th ed. New York: McGraw-Hill.

Samuelson, Paul A. 1954. The Pure Theory of Public Expenditure. *Review of Economics and Statistics* 36: 387–9.

Sandford, C. T., J. R. M. Willis, and D. J. Ironside. 1973. *An Accessions Tax*. London: Institute for Fiscal Studies.

Scanlon, T. M. 1975. Preference and Urgency. *Journal of Philosophy* 72: 655–69.

———. 1991. The Moral Basis of Interpersonal Comparisons. In *Interpersonal Comparisons of Well-being*, ed. Jon Elster and John E. Roemer, 17–44. Cambridge: Cambridge University Press.

———. 1998. *What We Owe to Each Other*. Cambridge, Mass. And London: Harvard University Press.

Scheffler, Samuel. 1982. *The Rejection of Consequentialism*. Oxford: Oxford University Press.

Schelling, Thomas. 1984. The Life You Save May Be Your Own. In Schelling, *Choice and Consequence*, 113–46. Cambridge, Mass.: Harvard University Press.

Schenk, Deborah H. 2000. Saving the Income Tax with a Wealth Tax. *Tax Law Review* 53: 423–75.

Schoenblum, Jeffrey A. 1995. Tax Fairness or Unfairness? A Consideration of the Philosophical Bases For Unequal Taxation of Individuals. *American Journal of Tax Policy* 12: 221–71.

Seligman, E. R. 1908. *Progressive Taxation in Theory and Practice*. 2nd ed. American Economic Association Quarterly, 3d series 9, no. 4.

Sen, Amartya K. 1977. Rational Fools: A Critique of the Behavioral Foundations of Welfare Economics. *Philosophy & Public Affairs* 6: 317–44.

———. 1985. The Moral Standing of the Market. *Social Philosophy and Policy* 2: 1–19.

———. 1997. *On Economic Inequality*. Enlarged ed., with James E. Foster. Oxford: Clarendon Press.

Shakow, David and Reed Shuldiner. 2000. A Comprehensive Wealth Tax. *Tax Law Review* 53: 499–584.

Shaviro, Daniel N. 1997. The Minimum Wage, the Earned Income Tax Credit, and Optimal Subsidy Policy. *University of Chicago Law Review* 64: 405–81.

———. 2000a. Inequality, Wealth, and Endowment. *Tax Law Review* 53: 397–421.

———. 2000b. *When Rules Change*. Chicago: University of Chicago Press.

Sidgwick, Henry. 1907. *The Methods of Ethics*. 7th ed. London: Macmillan.

Simons, Henry C. 1938. *Personal Income Taxation*. Chicago: University of Chicago Press.

Slemrod, Joel. 1990. Optimal Taxation and Optimal Tax Systems. *Journal of Economic Perspectives* 4: 157–78.

———. 1998. Methodological Issues in Measuring and Interpreting Taxable Income Elasticities. *National Tax Journal* 51: 773–88.

———, ed. 2000. *Does Atlas Shrug?* New York and Cambridge, Mass.: Russell Sage Foundation and Harvard University Press.

Slemrod, Joel and Jon Bakija. 2000. *Taxing Ourselves*. 2nd ed. Cambridge, Mass. and London: MIT Press.

———. Forthcoming. Does Growing Inequality Reduce Tax Progressivity? Should It? In Hassett and Hubbard (forthcoming).

Slemrod, Joel and Wojciech Kopczuk. Forthcoming. The Optimal Elasticity of Taxable Income. *Journal of Public Economics*.

Slemrod, Joel and Shlomo Yitzhaki. 2001. Integrating Expenditure and Tax Decisions: The Marginal Cost of Funds and the Marginal Benefit of Projects. *National Tax Journal* 54: 189–201.

Smith, Adam. 1789. *The Wealth of Nations*.

Stiglitz, Joseph E. 1987. Pareto Efficient and Optimal Taxation and the New New Welfare Economics. In *Handbook of Public Economics*, vol. 2, ed. Alan J. Auerbach and Martin Feldstein, 991–1042. Amsterdam: North-Holland.

———. 2000. *Economics of the Public Sector*. 3rd ed. New York: W. W. Norton.

Temkin, Larry S. 1993. *Inequality*. New York: Oxford University Press.

Tuomala, Matti. 1990. *Optimal Income Tax and Redistribution*. Oxford: Clarendon Press.

Vanistendael, Frans. 1996. Legal Framework for Taxation. In *Tax Law Design and Drafting*, vol. 1, ed. Victor Thuronyi, 15–70. Washington, D.C.: International Monetary Fund.

Van Parijs, Philippe. 1995. *Real Freedom For All*. Oxford: Clarendon Press.

Veblen, Thorstein. 1899. *The Theory of the Leisure Class*. New York: Macmillan.

Walker, Francis A. 1888. The Bases of Taxation. *Political Science Quarterly* 3: 1–16.

Warren, Alvin. 1980. Would a Consumption Tax Be Fairer Than an Income Tax? *Yale Law Journal* 89: 1081–1124.

Weisbach, David A. 2000. Ironing Out the Flat Tax. *Stanford Law Review* 52: 599–664.

Wicksell, Knut. 1896. A New Principle of Just Taxation. Reprinted in Musgrave and Peacock (1958), 72–118.

Wiggins, David. 1985. Claims of Need. In *Morality and Objectivity*, ed. Ted Honderich, 149–202. London: Routledge & Kegan Paul.

Witte, John F. 1981. Tax Philosophy and Income Equality. In *Value Judgement and Income Distribution*, ed. Robert A. Solo and Charles W. Anderson, 340–78. New York: Praeger.

Wolff, Edward N. 1996. *Top Heavy: The Increasing Inequality of Wealth in America and What Can Be Done about It.* New York: The New Press.

———. 2000. Recent Trends in Wealth Ownership, 1983–1998. Jerome Levy Economics Institute, Working Paper No. 300.

Woodman, Faye. 1988. The Tax Treatment of Charities and Charitable Donations Since the Carter Commission. *Osgoode Hall Law Journal* 26: 537–76.

Zelenak, Lawrence. 1993. Taxing Gains at Death. *Vanderbilt Law Review* 46: 361–441.

———. 1994. Marriage and the Income Tax. *Southern California Law Review* 67: 339–405.

———. 1999. The Selling of the Flat Tax: the Dubious Link Between Rate and Base. *Chapman Law Review* 2: 197–232.

Zelenak, Lawrence and Kemper Moreland. 1999. Can the Graduated Income Tax Survive Optimal Tax Analysis? *Tax Law Review* 53: 51–93.

Index

ability to pay, 20–30
accessions tax, 148, 156–9, 186
Ackerman, Bruce, 201n.66
aggregation, 52
Alstott, Anne L., 201n.66,
    206nn.26, 28, 207n.4,
    208n.12
Andrews, William, 101,
    199nn.21, 26, 29,
    200nn.40, 47
Aristotle, 9, 115, 191n.1
Armey, Dick, 100, 130–1,
    198n.10
Ascher, Mark L., 206n.22,
    207n.47
Atkinson, Anthony B.,
    194nn.20, 25, 196n.6
Auerbach, Alan J., 38, 196n.38
Auten, Gerald, 202n.81,
    204n.20

Bakija, Jon, 191n.3, 196nn.6,
    37, 198nn.6–7, 199nn.11,
    23, 202n.80, 203nn.7, 84,
    204nn.15, 17–8, 26

Bankman, Joseph, 118, 191n.3,
    199nn.22, 25, 200n.38,
    201nn.53, 57, 59, 62–3,
    204n.16
Becker, Gary S., 207n.45
Beitz, Charles, 198n.7
benefit principle, 16–9, 27
    restricted, 85
Bernstein, Jared, 204n.27
Bittker, Boris, 208n.7
Blattmachr, Jonathan G.,
    207n.50
Blum, Walter J., 131–2,
    193n.15, 194nn.28, 30,
    203n.9
Blumberg, Grace, 207n.4,
    208n.13
Bradford, David F., 14, 100,
    103–5, 145, 191n.3,
    192nn.8, 10, 194n.22,
    198nn.2–5, 8, 14, 16, 20–
    1, 29–30, 200nn.34–5, 46,
    201n.61, 202n.78, 203n.8,
    205n.18, 206n.19
Brown, Karen B., 207n.4